Good Intentions

and other Sermons that Matter

Mark Zimmerly

Parson's Porch Books

www.parsonsporchbooks.com

Good Intentions and other Sermons that Matter

ISBN: Softcover 978-1-949888-18-8

Copyright © 2018 by Mark Zimmerly

All rights reserved. No part of this book may be reproduced or transmitted in any form or by any means, electronic or mechanical, including photocopying, recording, or by any information storage and retrieval system, without permission in writing from the publisher.

Good Intentions

Contents

Sermons Matter..9

God's Multiverse 11
    Genesis 1

Full Stop..17
    Deuteronomy 5:12-15

Building Plans 22
    2 Samuel 7

Hidden Figures 28
    Daniel 3

Naboth's Vineyard 33
    1 Kings 21

Where is God? 39
    The Book of Esther

Spiritual Gifts 44
    Isaiah 62:1-5; 1 Corinthians 12:1-11

Good Intentions 49
    Amos 5

Let Justice Roll Down 55
    Amos 1-5

Message for the Captives...60
    Isaiah 61:1-11

The Good Gift..65
    Song of Songs

The Wisdom of God...71
    Proverbs 1: 20-33

Moving On 76
    Ruth 3-4

Mary, Did You Know? 82
  Luke 1:26-55
Emmanuel 87
  Luke 2:1-20
The Disturbing Word 89
  John 1
John the Baptist 94
  Luke 3:1-22
Rising to Serve 99
  Mark 1:29-39
Wanted 105
  Luke 15:1-32
Toward the Cross 110
  Luke 16
The Sheep and the Goats 116
  Matt 25:31-46
At Last 121
  John 2:1-11
Washing Feet 128
  John 13:1-17
Expect Nothing 134
  Luke 19:28-40
The Seven Last Words 139
  John 7
Beginning Again 142
  Mark 16:1-8
Paul and Silas in Prison 146
  Acts 16:16-34

Spiritual Jujitsu 152
    Philippians 4:1-9
Why Church? 157
    Hebrews 10
The Beast 163
    Revelation 13

Sermons Matter

Parson's Porch Books is delighted to present to you this series called Sermons Matter.

We believe that many of the best writers are pastors who take the role of preacher seriously. Week in, and week out, they exegete scripture, research material, write and deliver sermons in the context of the life of their particular congregation in their given community.

We further believe that sermons are extensions of Holy Scripture which need to be published beyond the manuscripts which are written for delivery each Sunday. Books serve as a vehicle for the sermon to continue to proclaim the Good News of the Morning to a broader audience.

We celebrate the wonderful occasion of the preaching event in Christian worship when the Pastor speaks, the People listen and the Work of the Church proceeds.

Take, Read, and Heed.

David Russell Tullock, M.Div., D.Min.
Publisher
Parson's Porch Books

God's Multiverse
Genesis 1

I'm glad you all could be here for this first Sunday in this new season of creation. We're starting over today in the Old Testament, and I'm looking forward to taking a new look at some stories of scripture this year, because it's different with each new reading, in part because of all the other things we read and experience between seasons.

For example, I finished a novel this past weekend that got me thinking about space and time and the nature of reality. It was a sci-fi thriller called *Dark Matter* by Black Crouch—not award-winning literature, but fun summer reading, for sure. The premise of the story, which is apparently based in real theoretical physics, and which I find fascinating is this:

Every time you or I make a decision, the reality we experience together continues in one direction, while in some other dimension, there is another reality in which another decision was made. So, with every word that is spoken, every step we take, every purchase we make, every relationship we pursue or deny, an alternate world is born, and from the decisions made in that world, additional alternate worlds branch off into infinite variations. Billions upon billions of realities in which there are different versions of ourselves, even, going in different directions based on the decisions they have made.

Now imagine opening a door into this multi-verse, which is a popular theme in fiction these days. Imagine being able to view or visit one of these alternate realities to see what could have been. Kind of like in Dickens' *Christmas Carol*, only without going forward or backward in time. In this theory, time is a constant. But imagine what life would be like for you now, if you had chosen a different school, or a different lover, or a different job. I think we all do this from time to time, don't we? Often when we're dreaming about greener pastures.

Fiction writers have done a good job of pointing out that many, if not most of those alternative realities would probably be horrific places. Like a world where nuclear war had broken out in the 80s. Or one in which the Nazis had won WWII. Imagine a world in which Donald Trump had won the presidency. Oh, right—that's the strange reality we now find ourselves in... It would be funny if it weren't true.

I remember Jesus saying once, "wide is the gate and broad is the road that leads to destruction, and many enter through it. But small is the gate and narrow the road that leads to life, and only a few find it." That's Matthew 7:13-14. When we consider the decisions of our lives and the realities of our world, we may wonder, are we on the wide road, or the narrow one?

Now consider Genesis 1. In the beginning. . . If the reality we know today is the product of an infinite number of small decisions, branching this way and that, at some point it should be possible to trace them back to a single point of origin. Maybe that's the big bang, maybe it's before space or time. Maybe we'll never know. But there was at least a time before human beings were able to make decisions—A or B. This way or that way. We couldn't decide because we didn't exist yet. There was a time before animals existed too. And before plants even. In the beginning, says this ancient story of our reality. In the beginning, there was only God. One being or life force capable of making a decision. And that God, for whatever reason, made a decision to create. Who knows—maybe there are other realities in which God made a different decision. But for some reason, in our reality, God made the world as we know it. I think that is remarkable—that God chose this world—this reality of ours somehow.

But more interestingly, God didn't just create the world as we see it today. God put into motion a reality which can go in an infinite number of different directions. Many if not most of which, are probably different than what God would have chosen. Think about that for a moment. God didn't just create this world. In some very important ways, God gave this reality the ability to create itself—to choose its own reality. And more importantly, we were given this ability. God gave us the space to do this.

It's easy to miss this aspect of the creation story, so I'll walk you through it in the text. We all remember how it starts, "Let there be light." And boom, there's light. But notice how on the next day—whatever a day meant in that space—in the second phase of creation, when God creates the sky or the atmosphere, God says "Let there be a dome in the midst of the water, and let it separate the waters from the waters." "Let it separate them." Says God. God doesn't separate the waters personally, God says, "Let the atmosphere take care of it." Which allows for the possibility of the atmosphere choosing not to. Suddenly, there's the possibility of a reality that God did NOT create. Can you imagine?

Now okay, okay, I get that this is unlikely because we don't think of the atmosphere as making its own decisions or being able to go in a different direction. But seemingly from the beginning, this is the pattern that God establishes in creation. God doesn't do it all herself/himself. On the third day God tells the waters to make space for land. God tells *the waters* to do this. Then God tells the land to bring forth vegetation. "Let the land bring forth vegetation." Says God. And it's not so much of a command as it is giving permission. "Let the land grow stuff, presumably, if the land wants to do it." God doesn't even specify the details of this vegetation besides that there be trees and seeds. And still, from that one command, all the vegetation of the earth evolves, in all its biodiversity, with its billions of permutations. At this point the length of a proverbial day still hasn't been determined, so we don't know exactly how long this takes, though I'm sure scientists have a good estimation of it.

In later epochs God tells the oceans to bring forth additional living creatures, and from these, eventually birds—all of which are told to be fruitful and multiply, to fill the earth. Note again that God doesn't do this personally—there's no intentional breeding going on here. It's left to the animals to work it out. The story goes that there was evening (as in an ending) and there was morning (as in a beginning). And in the 6th age of creation after God again tells the earth to bring forth a new set of wild creatures, God decides to make human beings in the likeness of God—female and male. And God tells them to rule over all the rest of creation. Implying that now our decisions will guide what happens to the cattle and the birds and the fish and the plants. And in that one act of creation, God chose to open a multiverse of beautiful, and horrific possibilities, because from the very beginning, we living creatures had the ability to say, "no!" We had the freedom to go a different way. Isn't that amazing! What an incredible risk God has taken on us, in giving us this freedom and responsibility. Can you believe that God trusted us enough to allow us to determine our own destiny? To shape our own world?

I find it amazing and a little crazy. To entrust a creation this elaborate and beautiful to a bunch of short-lived creatures, formed out of clay. And yet after doing this, God is so pleased with this decision that she/he/they decides to take a day off and just enjoy it. On the 7th day God rests from the work of creation, and this too is evidence of a kind of faith in us, the work of God's hands—that on God's day of rest we're not going to mess it all up. And yet it seems like that's exactly what happened. At this point in the story we're probably only talking about a day as we know them now—24 hours. But that's probably all it takes before Adam and Eve eat the apple, right? I'm picturing God giving the new couple their instructions on Friday afternoon, then going off on retreat after dinner. There's evening, there's morning. . . Then Saturday evening God is walking in the garden and can't find Adam. God says to them, "Why are you hiding from me? Did you eat that fruit that

I told you not to eat?" And the multiverse branches out even more exponentially from there.

This sounds like about the right time-line, right? A single day before we chose to go our own direction. And yet here's another point at which our Christian narrative is somewhat unique and remarkable. If I were God, and my creation chose a different path than the one I had intended for them, and I had access to the multiverse somehow, because essentially, I created it. I would probably choose to stick with the other couple. You know, the one that never ate the apple? I mean, wouldn't you choose that preferable reality? Or at the very least, I might wipe out those first people and try again. I'd say to the new ones, "Now you should know that I tried this with some other creatures, but they wouldn't listen, so. . ."

But that's not how this story goes. In our reality—the one you and I are still living with, God has chosen NOT to force us to do exactly what God wants us to do. From the very beginning of creation God wrote it into the fabric of our world, that we would have the freedom to make our own decisions—good or bad—no matter where they take us, and God has chosen to stick with us in the fallout from those decisions, even when our creative freedom leads us astray.

You could even say that this is the mystery of our faith—that God so loved the world, that instead of rejecting the world or destroying it, God loved it so much that God even came into it, taking the form of one of us. Not to condemn us for our sometimes-poor decisions, but instead to lead us into a better future, to make of us a new creation—a people forgiven and restored to life, capable once again of being co-creators with God.

Again, I remember the risen Jesus. The resurrected Christ who could somehow walk through walls and appear and disappear at will. The man called Jesus—meaning salvation—who said he was there at the creation of the world, and that he would stick with us to the end of it. I remember Jesus talking about there being many rooms in God's house. He said he goes to prepare a place for us there. So somehow, he is here and not here at the same time. I remember how he said to the thief on the cross—today you will be with me in paradise. The Kingdom of God is somehow here now, but also not yet arrived. That kind of stuff used to sound a bit strange to me sometimes. Magical. Surreal. But now when I read about the science of dark matter and subatomic particles and string theory, I consider our scriptures and I marvel that it was written down so long ago. I wonder if someday all of this will make perfect sense in ways that we can scarcely imagine now.

But in the meantime, there's one thing I know for sure, and this creation narrative affirms it. Our decisions matter. God has given us the freedom and responsibility to help shape our reality, with every choice that we make. Where we live, what we buy, who we welcome. Every action or inaction, it makes a difference on a cosmic level, because we are God's partners in creation. Therefore, Paul writes in the book of Romans that all of creation waits in eager longing for the revealing of the children of God. Because God also intends to save the world with us and through us. During this reality—the one that you and I are living here and now.

So, we know our purpose in this world. We know what direction we are to go—to become people of decisive and creative action. No matter what poor decisions have been made in the past, no matter how much we wish our current reality were different—as individuals, as a nation, we can take solace in the fact that God is with us in this reality, still calling us to live into a new creation, where justice flows down like waters, righteousness like an ever flowing stream. Therefore, let us be strong and courageous, especially when others try to take our world in a bad direction.

When some governors and the trump administration say we should deport people who have no other home. We can choose to take the stranger and the immigrant into our homes and into our lives, to protect them as God in Christ has protected us.

When representatives of the White House try to change the narrative of our country—saying the Statue of Liberty wasn't originally a beacon of welcome, we can respond by creating a new narrative—one in which our country is now called to be a place of welcome, a place of refuge—a place where we work together to create a better world for all God's children.

And this kind of creation can have cosmic implications. As human beings pollute the earth to the point of changing the very climate, and we start to feel the effects of this destruction through more frequent hurricanes, through floods and droughts, and famine. We can respond to this destruction by becoming again agents of creation. Not just rebuilding after national disasters but coming up with creative ways to reduce greenhouse gas emissions and protect ecosystems and equip people around the world to live in harmony with nature, rather than destroy it.

And as we do this work of creation, we do so in the image of God, the creator. We do it in partnership with the Holy Spirit, our sustainer—the one who breathes inspiration into us and helps us to keep running the race even when it feels like we're losing. And we do this work of creation with God the Human One, who came that we might have life, and life to its full!

I invite you to consider again the multi-verse. The thousands of possibilities of what could have been. Now hear again the good news of the gospel, that God has chosen to be with us in this reality. In this time and this place. Again, and again and again, no matter how many wrong turns we may have taken in the past, God is with us still to reform us and reshape us into a new creation, God's own people, filled with faith, hope, and love, for the life of the world.

Full Stop
Deuteronomy 5:12-15

Well, I have some bad news for you all this morning. Summer in Seattle is pretty much over. I know we technically have a few more weeks before September 21st, and we could get some nice weather still, but Labor Day is the end of vacation season for most people. Once the schools are back in session, that's it. We wave goodbye to our neighbors and prepare for another nine months of rain. Back on the treadmill, back to the grind.

And oh, how we'll miss those wonderfully lazy summer days! Days for hiking, biking, camping, sailing, hanging out on the lake, shooting the breeze, laying in hammocks, enjoying that patio at the coffee shop or the pub or your own back-yard. Raise your hand if you had a vacation this season! How about a staycation? Good for you! According to takebackyourtime.org, most Americans didn't take all their vacation last year, even though 9 out of 10 of us say our happiest memories come from vacations. So, a lot of people are missing out.

I invite you to relish those vacation memories for a moment this morning. Since a good measure of happiness is derived from remembering good times and relishing those memories--let's do that together. I invite you to think back to a good moment from this summer. Think of a time when you felt really relaxed. Or maybe it wasn't relaxed—maybe you felt joyful or exited. I took my kids to Wildwaves this summer and it wasn't relaxing, but man it was fun. That's a great memory for me. Remember a time when you felt carefree, and just grateful to be alive. Remember how it felt to be in that moment, fully present. Whatever you were doing or not doing, how it just felt so good! Maybe you were in a hot tub. Maybe you were sun bathing, maybe you were sky diving or skinny dipping or reading a book. Maybe you were with friends or family. Maybe you were alone. Just remember how that felt. How it felt in your body. What it was like for your mind, to be in that space. Are you there? Can you see it? Can you remember it?

Now imagine feeling that way at least once every week. Every single week. One day a week. 52 days a year! And imagine that God wants this time for you, this space for you, so much that God commanded that you take it. Made it a commandment! As in "though shalt do this" whether you want to or not. That's Sabbath. Isn't that freaking awesome? Can you believe that we worship a God that demands this kind of blessing? Not just occasionally, as in 10 vacation days a year—if you can fit it in—kind of thing, but every single week. Benjamin Franklin once said that beer is proof that God loves us and wants us to be happy, but I think it's Sabbath that proves this. It's Sabbath that gives us the room to be still and know that God is. To taste and see that the Lord is good. It's such an amazingly good gift.

And yet people resist it. We all resist it just like we resist the rest of the commandments. It's sad and ironic how we run from Sabbath rest, but we do. There seems to be something in us, or at least something at work in the world that makes us resist God's good intentions for us. We take all the things that God gives us to make us happy and we twist them around to make ourselves unhappy. It makes no sense, but that's the way things are. I see this with my children all the time. It doesn't seem to matter what I give them—Legos, cotton candy, a sock monkey. "Look, Dad, I built a sword—and it fits in my nose!" or "Dad, his scoop is bigger than mine—it's not fair!" or I look over and the sock monkey is abusing the cat. Not okay!

"Stop!" I say. "That's enough!" "No more of that!" Maybe the gift must go away for a while, or the child must take some time away to think about the cat's feelings.

That's what the word Sabbath means, by the way. It means "Stop." Or "Cease." The whole restful part is just implied, because if you stop whatever it is you're doing, you are essentially resting from that activity. It's like how modern parenting encourages us to deal with the Sock Monkey problem. We're meant to say, "Ok, it sounds like the sock monkey needs to rest now. He's going to take a little break." Which is much better than saying "Stop it!" even if the reaction is pretty much the same. Kids will still whine and cry if you take away their toys, but it's good for them to learn to take breaks occasionally.

And for some reason we must continue to be reminded of this as adults. God says to us pretty much the same thing—"hey, I know you're enjoying all the things you've been doing throughout the week—at least I hope you have been, but even good things can become a problem when you get too much of them, so it's time to give it a rest already!" Too much work, too much TV, even too much vacation is possible. Some of us party so hard in the summertime, going from BBQ to BBQ, letting the sun bring out our extroverted sides, that when the weather finally turns, we're a bit relieved. That's when you know you're a true Seattleite—when the rain comes back and you're like, "ahhh, finally I just get to sit in my house and read a book!" That's Sabbath too. Anybody with me?

But imagine living in healthy balance all year long, no matter what the weather. Imagine having the permission—and more than that—the requirement—to celebrate God's gifts in moderation, every week of the year by setting aside one day in seven to stop them. What would you stop doing if you had the chance? Better yet, what do you think God would want you to take a break from? I bet you know already. I've already mentioned a bunch of options this morning and we all have things we need to stop doing, so what's one thing that you can or should probably let go of one day a week? I put a stop sign in the back of your bulletin, since that's what Sabbath means "Stop." I invite you to write something in or next to that stop sign that would probably be good for you to stop. It could be something traditional—a lot of people give up shopping or cleaning or checking email on the Sabbath since these are things that tend to be stressful and feel like work. But it could be something a bit less work related. Like maybe on that one day a week, God would want you to stop drinking or planning your next vacation or checking the stock market or listening to the news. Write something down. And then write a day of the week, and then take this home and tape this to your bathroom mirror. See if that helps.

You might change your mind at some point about what stopping looks like for you. And that's okay too. A good way to go about it, is to start to notice what feels oppressive in your life. What is it that feels compulsive, restrictive—what is it that keeps you from enjoying God's good creation? What keeps you from being in God's presence, from just being happy to be alive? This text from the book of Deuteronomy links the Sabbath to the Israelite's experience of deliverance from slavery. When the people of God were slaves in Egypt, they were forced to work seven days a week, so that was their problem. God set them free from slavery so that they could stop working, one day a week—that's Sabbath. So, what is it that we need to be set free from in our 24/7 culture? For some it's still workaholism—thinking about or doing work every day of the week, but for most of us it's something else.

I read about one practice common in some Jewish families—they have something called a Sabbath box—it's just a box that sits next to the front door. And at the beginning of the Sabbath, everyone in the family puts something in the box that they aren't going to use for 24 hours. These days it might include cell phones, laptops, game consoles, car keys. Then at the end of the Sabbath, they take those things out. Simple, right? Some people—most of us—watch way more TV than is good for us. Our flat screen TVs might not fit in a box by the door, but how about the remote? Or the power cord? Or the internet router?

I know at this point some of you are probably getting a bit nervous. Even talking about taking breaks from some of these things can be anxiety producing. But that's sort of the point. We're never going to be able to completely do away with the stuff in our lives that tends to control us, but part what stopping them regularly does for us is it helps us to recognize the ways we start to idolize certain behaviors and activities—the way we live as though we can't do without them. So, the Sabbath is a way of re-asserting our God given freedom from addictive behaviors. It's a way of helping ourselves to see that yes, I can stop. And sometimes it makes it so that over time we will stop more permanently. Not just stop being glued to our screens all the time, but it might mean stopping ignoring our friends or family. It might mean ceasing to neglect prayer and worship or scripture. Sabbath might help us to let go of our constant distracted, multi-tasking way of being in the world so that we can pay attention to matters of justice and respond to them. This is the gift God has in store for us when we say yes to God's command to stop. Sometimes we have to give up some good activities in order to engage in even better ones.

Here's a sports analogy for you. I know you're all leaning in now—Mark is attempting a sports analogy! Don't get too excited—it's not so much about the guys on the field. I noticed that when you go to watch a sporting event, there's a lot of wasted time. Have you noticed this? Baseball and football, I find mind-numbingly boring because for every second of playtime it feels like there are several minutes where nothing is happening. They're between plays or between innings and you get up to get some garlic fries, and oops! --you missed the touch-down because they got the injured player off the field earlier than you thought they would. I used to think that the whole thing would be better if they just set a timer and called it done after an hour or so. But then I started going to games. And seeing people in the stands talking to each other. And I noticed the funny little traditions that go on between plays with the cartoon speed boat races and the screens showing people kissing and waving and singing. Now, for me, it's the stoppage time that makes the games palatable. That's when the relationships happen! That's when you get to enjoy your food. That's when you get to just relax and enjoy yourself, instead of worrying about whether your team is going to make it to the playoffs. It puts the whole game in perspective. Sabbath is like that. You must stop sometimes in order to appreciate the rest of the action.

Are you convinced yet? Is Sabbath starting to feel like a practice worth investing in? I know it can be a hard concept to embrace—that less is more, that sometimes doing nothing is worth doing. It flies in the face of our hyper-productive, competitive, results-based culture. And it doesn't help that previous generations have sometimes dealt poorly with this commandment. I know some people may have memories of legalistic Sabbath practice—the kind Jesus got upset about. How some people thought that the fourth commandment was about stopping anything enjoyable as a way of showing our obedience to God. But that's just a way that people managed to twist even the good command of Sabbath into something oppressive. Jesus wasn't having any of that. Notice that Jesus came not to do away with Sabbath—not to abolish this law, but to fulfill it—to show us how to do it right! When Jesus celebrated Sabbath, he made a point of eating and drinking in celebration of God's good gifts, because Sabbath is meant to be a joyful celebration! We are free not to work 24/7—halleluiah. We are free to take vacations. We are free to let our employees and our devices and our communities rest. When Jesus celebrated Sabbath, he healed people, because Sabbath is meant to be healing, restorative—it's meant to put things back in their righteous and just place! So, if you love to clean on the Sabbath, go for it! If it gives you joy to binge watch a Netflix show on the Sabbath—you are free to do that too. God bless you! Because Sabbath isn't about creating new obligations or enforcing old ones. It's just about stopping, one day a week to celebrate. Still today the Lord of the Sabbath is calling us to stop, in some way, shape or form one day a week—a 24-hour period. We are meant to live differently on that day somehow—so that this day is different, set apart, holy. So that we can be blessed, healed, re-created, made whole and new once a week. Will you give it a shot? Will you embrace the freedom we have in Christ to NOT do something? All you must do is Stop. One day a week. Just give it a rest already.

Building Plans
2 Samuel 7

A few weeks ago, I was lounging around in my basement on a Sabbath afternoon, escaping the ridiculous heat that takes over the upstairs of my house on days like today. And while I was laying around down there, I found some old picture albums that I hadn't looked through in years. The pictures were back from the days before everybody had smartphones and Facebook was still brand new, so people took the time to print photo albums. You remember that? It was only about 10 years ago. That was a reminder of how life has changed. But then I was surprised to look at the pictures and see myself as an almost totally different person. Has that ever happened to you too?

What a different life I had, just a decade ago--how different my hopes and dreams and expectations had been. In 2004 I remember I was working at a place called the Campbell Farm in Eastern Washington on the Yakama Indian reservation. They grew apples there, but it wasn't so much of a farm as a mission support station where church groups would come to learn and to do service projects. In the evenings I worked with a Native American youth group, playing songs on my guitar and leading silly games. During the day I led chores and organized trips and built stuff. They called me Captain Compost, because my favorite activity was introducing Jr high & high school students to the miracle of God's little recyclers.

Man, I loved that job! I loved working on the farm, I felt at home in the Yakama culture. I loved it so much that I was convinced that was where I would spend the rest of my life. Composting, growing apples, serving people in need, "Caring for God's creation from the ground up." I went away to seminary in the fall, but even in 2015 I still had all sorts of plans for what I would do in Wapato when I got back. I was going to repair old buildings and build new uber-sustainable ones with straw bales and tires. I even had a design in mind for a new worship space--a sanctuary dug into the ground like a retreat center I had visited in Northern Ireland once, designed to mimic the layout of the inner ear. I had beautiful dreams, some of them ambitious, maybe a little bit grandiose. And yet in the end, it was clear that God had said no. God said no to my dreams! It took me years to figure it out, to be able to hear it and accept that it wasn't going to happen, but eventually--now more than 10 years later, I know that God wasn't supportive of my plans to go back to the Campbell Farm. They may have been good plans--It may have just been that I wasn't the person to carry out those plans--someone else would do it. In the end the problem was that it was something I wanted to do, just not necessarily what God wanted for me.

Have you had anything like that in your life? A dream canceled, a plan given over to a different person or a different generation or a different world altogether? We can spend a lot of time and energy hoping and planning for futures that never comes to pass. And it is so disappointing! Job opportunities that are missed. Partners and lovers that are never found, or who are found wanting. Children who never come, or who come out differently than we had hoped. And I think our disappointment is greatest when we believe our plans are ones God would approve of. Careers that build up God's kingdom. Healthy families that glorify God. Sometimes our friends and community members encourage us, pray for us, saying, "surely God is with you, don't give up." But then for some reason, still God says no! And we're like, "Really? Seriously God, what gives?"

Today's installment from the Samuel Series is good illustration of this gap between our plans and God's providence, and of the simple fact that our ways are not always God's ways. Interestingly it is the center of the David story of 1st and 2nd Samuel. Biblical scholars seem to agree that this little interaction is set up to be the most important message in the whole saga--it encapsulates the main theme of these books of history, so it's a story worth revisiting.

At this point in the narrative King David has come to a place of relative stability--for the time being he has peace from his enemies both within and beyond the kingdom of Israel. And David is grateful to God for bringing him to this position, so in gratitude, David decides to build God a temple. Which seems like a very good thing, don't you think? It's almost exactly what we still hope to do in worship--how in gratitude for all that God has done for us, we seek to bless God, and sometimes this means contributing to the building of worship spaces--there's nothing wrong with that! Go for it, David, we say! And David's process here isn't all that bad either. David doesn't just build the temple and then say, "here you go, God." First David goes to the prophet Nathan to check in and make sure he's doing good discernment. Wherever two or three agree on something, right? And it turns out that Nathan also thinks this is a great idea. "Go ahead," says Nathan, "For Surely-- God is with you."

But then that night something unexpected happens. God comes to Nathan and says to him basically, "Wait a minute. I know you two guys think this makes sense, but I'm not into it. I've been doing just fine living in a tent for generations now. If I'd wanted a permanent building, I would have asked for one already. But thanks anyway." That's pretty much the answer to David's dreams of a temple. God says, "No thanks."

Which is certainly puzzling response for those of us reading it after the fact. I mean, why isn't David the right person to build the temple? In this version of the story, no explanation is given. Which makes it seem a bit unfair even. If it were me, I'd be asking "Why?" Why not a building? Why can't David build one? Is it an ego thing, is it an opportunity cost issue? So often we want to know, when God says, no, we want to know the reasoning. Couldn't God not be a little more specific?

It is particularly strange considering how God goes on to say that David can't build the temple, but his son someday will! What's with that? Clearly, it's not simply that God hates building projects. God may have been fine living in a tent for hundreds of years, but it wasn't the plan forever, so why a building later but not now? Why does God give opportunities and privileges to others that are sometimes denied to us? Did God simply want David to have asked more directly? To have spent more time in prayer? We could spend years trying to get to the bottom of why God works the way God does, but in the end sometimes all we get is silence. "God's ways are not our ways." Often our plans simply aren't God's plans, and the reality is that God is the one in charge.

Which sounds like a pretty rotten deal if the story ends there. If all we get is a "No" from God when we try to do good things. But that's why we also need to listen for God's alternative. It turns out there is a second part to this covenant between God and David, and in the end, David doesn't come out all that bad off. God says to David, "You're not the one to build the temple, David. But! Because you've sought to bless me. Because you've agreed to go along with my plans instead of your own, I'm going to bless YOU. I'm going to build YOU a house, and the kind of house I'm going to build isn't the kind you could build for yourself. Because I'll make sure your household continues forever, and that of your descendants there will be no end." That's the deal God makes with David--the one that is at the center of the narrative about David. God says to him, "You don't get to bless me, I get to bless you--I'm the one who calls the shots, I'm the one who builds the house." Get it?

To his credit, David certainly gets it. He'll take God's blessing over a building campaign any day. So, what if he doesn't get to put his name on a plaque, God has promised to bless his family forever, no matter what they do or don't do. Isn't that a better deal?

Good Intentions

Amazingly it's the same deal God gives to us too. If we're willing to take it. The gospel of Matthew makes a point of this with its long genealogy of Jesus. Matthew points out that there were 14 generations between God's promise to Abraham and God's promise to David. First God said to Abraham, I will make your descendants as numerous as the stars in the sky, and they, like you, will be blessed to be a blessing to all the people of the earth. Then 14 generations later, God affirms a new promise to Abraham's descendant David, saying I will now bless your descendants, even if they abandon me. Even if they fall short, I will still uphold them, says God. 14 generations later, after the temple that was later build for God was destroyed, God told the people exiled in Babylon that the promise was still good: a descendant of David was still coming, to bless all the people of the earth. And though they had to wait another 14 generations, that savior did come. A descendant of David named Jesus, who referred to himself as the temple, the house of God, the one that even if destroyed would be resurrected to bless all the peoples of the earth--of this new kingdom there would be no end. This new "Son of David" waded into crowds of God's people, saying to them things like, "Blessed are you when you are disappointed. When you are frustrated, broken, worn down by the turns your life has taken. Because, like David, that's when you are free to see God at work to bless you in unexpected ways! That's when you find out that it's not about your plans or expectations--it's about God's provision." Jesus said to them, "Come to me, all you who are weary and heavy laden--burdened by plans of your own making, and I will give you rest, I will build you an even better hope and future. Abide in me and my commands, he said, and I will abide in you. Come follow me and I will graft you into my family, the likes of which has no end." Even when Jesus was on his way to heaven, he said to them and to us, "I go to prepare a house for you. I prepare the house for you. So, don't be worried. Don't be afraid, no matter what happens."

Often, we try to bless God, and instead God blesses us! We try to make good plans and carry out good projects, but God says no because there is already a better plan underway. We don't always get to see the blueprints for these plans, but we can trust the architect. Even if it takes another 14 generations to realize the fullness of the Beloved Community, we know we are on our way because God is building the house. Jesus our carpenter is framing in the walls and laying down the roof and carving beautiful welcome signs for the doors to our rooms. And all we must do is to say, "thank you." "Thank you, God, for not abandoning us to our own plans and projects. For not letting us get distracted from your absolute call on our lives. Thank you for housing us, for sheltering us again and again, no matter how often we run away. We will gladly live with your rules and follow in your ways if it means we get to stay. For better is one day in your courts than a thousand elsewhere. In your house is a better life than anything we could have built or even imagined for ourselves.

I've been reading a novel this summer that is worth reading even though it is ridiculously long. It's called a Soldier of the Great War by Mark Helprin. Anyone else read it? The novel follows the life of an Italian man named Allesandro in the first world war. In the beginning you read about his early life, Allesandro's formative experiences, the people he loves, his hopes and dreams for the future, then you get to watch as the war slowly takes all of these things from him, one my one, until he has nothing left but his own life--until all his dreams are gone. It sounds depressing, but what's surprising about the novel though is that it is still upbeat, because Allesandro remains heroic throughout the fighting, never letting his losses get him down. When he returns from the war, there is a scene where he is sitting at a beach watching families with young children playing. He ends up talking to a man who reminds him of a friend he lost in the war. Allesandro remembers the dreams he used to have of love and of children, for building his garden that is now also lost. He realizes he could be jealous of these happy people who somehow came through the war unscathed. He could be bitter that God didn't go along with his plans for a family, for his own happily ever after. He could be bitter, but instead all he has left is gratitude. He could be jealous, but instead Allesandro sees nothing but beauty in the lives of the people around him, and he allows this to bring him a small measure of joy. Allesandro finds hope in the fact that he gets to be a part of this larger story of life, marred as it is by disappointment and pain. The beauty of the world will go on according to God's plan--and this is worth celebrating, no matter what happens.

Friends, most of us don't have to mourn the losses of every dream and person we've ever loved. But we all have something we have to let go of in order to let God embrace us more fully. It can be a great ambition, or it can be as simple as not being able to spend more time composting. Whatever it is for you, I urge you to put it in God's hands again this morning. Trust that God has something even better in store for you, even if your joy is slow in coming, know that it will come. For the God who loved David, also loves you through our Lord Jesus Christ. God loves you more than you can ever imagine. And God's dreams for you will never end.

I invite you pray with me. And as you do, I invite you to picture whatever dream you've lost in your life. Hold it like this, with a clenched fist. And as we pray, slowly open your hand and imagine letting it go. Imagine giving to God all of your disappointment and frustration and accepting it its place the joy of those who have been promised eternal habitations.

Let us pray: Lord we know that you have had plans for us since before we were even born. You have had plans to prosper and not to harm us. Plans to give us also a hope and a future better than the ones we have sometimes had in mind for ourselves. Help us, Lord, to trust in you with all of our hearts and not to lean too much on our own understanding. Help us to seek first your kingdom and its righteousness, trusting that all these other things we long for will be given to us as well, in your time-- homes and siblings and parents and children and gardens--all these things we put in your hands, for the sake of your gospel and of your son Jesus in whose name we pray. Amen.

Hidden Figures
Daniel 3

Today's story is a familiar one for those who grew up going to Sunday School because it's a popular children's story. Shadrach, Meshach and Abednego. Even if you can't remember the names, it's hard to forget the image of the blazing furnace, and the fourth figure walking around in the fire with these men who refused to bow down to the giant statue. They put their bodies on the line to stand up for a higher law, and God saved them from the fire. Great story—Shadrach, Meshach, and Abednego. I wish I could remember how the song goes. . . it's been too long.

But then again, these names in the song are part of the problem, so maybe they are better forgotten. You see Shadrach, Meshach, and Abednego weren't these guy's real names at all. You have to read from the beginning of the book of Daniel to learn that their given names in Hebrew were Hananiah, Mishael and Azariah, but they were given new names by their slave-masters when they were taken as captives to Babylon as young men. The King who later had them thrown in a fiery furnace for refusing to bow down to a statue, first gave them names honoring the Babylonians gods—one of many ways to try to make them assimilate into Babylonian culture and leave their old religion behind.

The King also ordered that they go to a special school, where they would be taught in the language of the empire and forced to abandon the culture and customs of their ancestors. It would have been kind of like the schools that Native American children were once sent to in this country and in Canada—where education was used as an instrument of systemic subjugation and oppression. The American empire, not unlike the Babylonian empire, has always claimed to support the freedom of religion. But only if that religion speaks our language. . . and allows for oil drilling in sacred lands. And doesn't mind fishing practices that destroy sacred animals. If that religion doesn't conflict with capitalism, or missionary activity, or national defense, or other hallmarks of the American way of life.

So, what's remarkable first about the immigrants in this story is the way that they manage to succeed and get ahead even during this oppressive environment. They remind me of those who were until recently part of the DACA program—those immigrants who arrived as children not knowing the language, not having the advantages of wealth or citizenship, a surprising number of whom learned to thrive in school and went on to make incredible contributions to their adopted country. People like Jose and Jorge and Miguel. Now known of course as Joe and George and Michael. Good guys.

It's amazing to see what people can do during this kind of adversity. Shadrach, Meshach and Abednego did seem willing to give up, or at least hide, some of their cultural identity in order to fit in to the empire, but at the same time they held on to what they could. Earlier in the book of Daniel we learn about their dietary habits. Rather than eat the rich Babylonian foods that would have been against the dietary laws of Leviticus, they chose to go vegetarian in Babylon. No meat or wine, just vegetables and water. And the story says they became healthier because of this restriction! I wonder if that's part of what helped them to get ahead—it surely at least helped them to stick together, these cultural outcasts. It reminds me of Jewish people in this country who choose the vegetarian option in order to stay Kosher at public events, or Muslim people from other countries who may adopt English names but continue to eat Halal. Thank God that at least the American empire doesn't force people to eat hamburgers and hot-dogs. America isn't always thrilled about hijabs or yarmulkes, but you can be vegetarian if you want to. There's that.

So, Shadrach, Meshach, and Abednego, because of their principles and discipline, and honesty, and hard work, they rise to secure top jobs in the government. The King himself notes that these guys are wiser than all the other officials of his kingdom. But they're still captives from Judah. They're still Hebrews. The situation reminds me of those women from NASA. You were wondering when I was going to get there, weren't you? Hopefully you've seen that movie, Hidden Figures, or maybe read the book. It's a story of resistance, just like the book of Daniel, where these smart African-American women are so brilliant at math and hardworking and respectable that they are brought to work on the national space program during the Jim Crow era. Even the top people at NASA must admit that these women are smarter than anyone else in the whole agency, but they're still women, and they're still black. So, they still must tow that line.

One of the things that was so amazing about that film was the way that those talented women composed themselves during that oppressive situation. Did you all notice that? How respectful and calm they were—the way they had to be. How they had to be above reproach, even when running for miles to the bathroom or facing constant insults? Today we may thank God that Jim Crow is behind us—the color line has shifted-- but why is it that African-Americans still must be above reproach with police officers in this country, lest they be shot? Why do Muslims and Sikhs and pretty much all refugees have to behave better than everyone else, just to get ahead in this society? Just to make it? Just to survive?

Well, this is the way of empire. It's been that way since Babylon. And in this story from scripture, this story of resistance, there finally comes a point when Hananiah, Mishael and Azariah aren't willing to take it anymore. The king makes a law that everyone must bow down before some silly statue, and these dignified men decide that they've had enough. New names? Fine, they say. Language? Okay. But break one of the basic commandments of the creator—one of the big 10? Not gonna happen. "Over my dead body"—that's their conviction. The king tells these men directly, like some evil slave-master in the confederate south, he says, "you better bow down or you're going to burn—what God do you think will save you?" But Hananiah, Mishael and Azariah stand their ground, and reply simply and respectfully as they always do. "O King" they say, "Maybe our God will save us, but even if that doesn't happen, still we will not bow down to your statue or serve your gods."

And the rest, as they say, is history. God saves them from the fire and King Nebuchadnezzar is so amazed that he gives the men a promotion and declares that the God of the Hebrews is to be respected throughout his empire. He says of Hananiah, Mishael and Azariah admiringly, "These men were willing to offer up their very bodies rather than worship other gods." Can you believe that? Even this despicable king comes to see the immigrant captives as heroes of faith. Isn't that something? Can you imagine our commander --in chief honoring subjugated peoples in this way? You'd think he could have at least mustered something similar for the famous native American code talkers this last week, but no. What an empire we live in that this Babylonian King from scripture appears more sensible than our democratically elected leader in America!

We live in a challenging context today. So, the story of these three brave non-violent resistors leaves me with a significant question: What are we willing to offer up our bodies for? What part of our identity is so important to us that we would be willing to die to protect it? What is the line we will not cross? What is the law of God that we will not break? I realize that's four questions, but you get the idea. Do we have these kinds of convictions, these sacred ideals, or have we just become part of the empire—the one that supports oppressive laws and offensive leaders?

It happens that this story of the men in the fire is mentioned by Martin Luther King Jr. in his Letter from a Birmingham jail. MLK explains his call to civil disobedience as being in this biblical tradition of Daniel, as well as in line with those Christians who were martyred for maintaining their faith under the Roman Empire, and those who stood against Hitler's German Empire. I notice that Rev Dr. King often had to defend his work for civil rights, not just religious freedom--but also for the dignity and freedom of all oppressed people. Let it be remembered that he was working on the poor people's campaign—organizing for worker justice when he was assassinated.

Well how many people in this century are willing to put their lives on the line for that kind of conviction? Who among us people of faith will stand against unjust actions of our nation because, like Hananiah, Mishael and Azariah we believe we too are accountable to a higher law—the law of our creator to do justice for all God's children?

Dr King went on to write that he had become disappointed with those who were unwilling to take a stand and risk something on behalf of brothers and sisters in need—particularly white moderates. He wrote,

"I have almost reached the regrettable conclusion that the Negro's great stumbling block in his stride toward freedom is not the White Citizen's councilor or the Ku Klux Klanner, but the white moderate, who is more devoted to "order" than to justice; who prefers a negative peace which is the absence of tension to a positive peace which is the presence of justice; who constantly says: "I agree with you in the goal you seek, but I cannot agree with your methods of direct action";

Rev Dr. King was someone who, like Hananiah, Mishael, and Azariah, willing to put his own body on the line in order to bring forth justice. He was willing to face the furnace because of his belief in a higher law given to him by the God of all Creation. Dr King sometimes felt called to break the unjust laws of the empire because the God he served came down from heaven to do exactly that. Just like Hananiah, Mishael and Azariah, Jesus came among us as one who, while respectful and honest and faithful in all things, chose to seek first God's kingdom and its justice. So, he healed on the Sabbath. And he told truth to people who didn't like to hear it. Jesus criticized unjust systems and one time even physically evicted some bankers who were exploiting the poor. Jesus lived for a higher law, and he was unapologetic about it. Because of this they dragged him before the governor—a guy named Pilot who asked Jesus why he shouldn't have him executed. And Jesus made no defense. Just like those original resistors who said to King Nebuchadnezzar, "We have no need to defend ourselves." Jesus faced the heat willingly because he trusted in God's judgment and deliverance.

And the rest, again, is history. The Roman empire fell, but Jesus rose from the dead and continues to lead a kingdom that will never end—it's a Beloved Community upheld by people like Martin Luther King Jr and all who choose to trust in God and live by a higher law.

I think we hear these stories sometimes and we think, "hey that's great for them, but I'm no Martin Luther King Jr. I'm no hero of faith. I'm not Hananiah, Mishael or Azariah. And I'm certainly not Jesus." But keep in mind that none of these people were looking to be heroes to begin with. And they certainly weren't trying to get killed. These people of faith were simply being faithful. For the captives from Judah it started with their diet. Choosing to eat in a way that was glorifying to God. For Dr King it started with a bus boycott. They asked him to help get some justice in transportation, and he said okay.

Well what would it look like to work for justice in our transportation system today? Or how about our global food system? Is anyone paying attention to what's going on at the port of Seattle these days, or with restaurant workers? My sense is that we don't have to look very far to find injustice in our society—to see our neighbors being oppressed. The question still is how much are we willing to put up with? Where do we draw the line? Jesus summarized the true law as that of loving God *and loving neighbor*. So, are we willing to face the fire of controversy for the sake of our neighbors? Are we willing to say for example, YES, I'll take the homeless poor into my house—it may be dangerous, but this is the law of God! Or might we protect the stranger and the immigrant—even shielding them from the authorities, because this too is God's higher law of hospitality? Today there are faithful people of many different religious backgrounds who are standing against unjust building projects and excessive incarceration, heartless evictions, environmental exploitation, gender bias in the workplace. Will we stand with them? Will we risk our time, our money, our lives?

This is no children's story, friends. The consequences both of action and inaction are as real for us as they were for Hananiah, Mishael, and Azariah. So, hear this word from scripture—in the end it is those who enter the furnace who are saved. That's where the blessing comes from. And when we are willing to go to that place—and face the heat, we find that we are not alone. God is with us in that uncomfortable place, even during that hellish fire, to keep us cool, calm and collected. And to bring us back out—to safety, to an even greater life-- for the Glory of God and the protection of God's people. Jesus said to us, in this world you will have trouble, but take heart, for I have overcome the world!

Naboth's Vineyard
1 Kings 21

There's a scene in the TV show "Better Call Saul" that reminds me of a dynamic in today's story from the Old Testament. The scene is a flash-back, letting us in on the back story for the protagonist of the show—a morally challenged attorney named Jimmy McGill. When Jimmy was a kid his father owned a gas station with a convenience store, where father and son were often behind the counter together. Well one day a guy comes into the store asking for some help because, he says, his car has broken down and he's out of money, and his wife is pregnant, etc. etc. Jimmy says to his Dad— "don't give him anything, dad, he's lying, I can tell." But Jimmy's Dad helps the stranger out anyway and scolds his son for being so rude. When the dad goes into the back room looking for some diapers to give to the man in need, however, the stranger pulls a gun and demands that Jimmy give him the money in the cash register. In the process the robber takes some time to level with this little boy. He says to him, "Kid, I can see you've got some sense, so let me give you some advice. There are two types of people in this world. There are sheep, and there are wolves. Your dad is a sheep. I'm a wolf. In the end the sheep get taken. You decide which you're going to be." And with that he walks casually out the door with the cash, never to be seen again. With this advice in mind, Jimmy then seems to decide he'd rather be a wolf than a pushover like his father.

It's a sad story. And unfortunately, somewhat true to life. Sometimes we do see the wicked prosper while the righteous suffer, and it really makes you wonder if there is no justice, and if it wouldn't be better to be a wolf after-all. That's the problem with this story of Naboth's vineyard as well. It's not a well-known story from scripture, probably for this reason. It makes us uncomfortable. We see a wicked King, King Ahab, and his wife Jezebel—they conspire to get an innocent man killed because they want his land and he's not willing to sell it. Ahab and Jezebel covet and steal and murder and bear false witness—an assortment of 10 commandment "thou shalt nots." And they do it all just because Ahab wants Naboth's property as a garden. Not even because he needs it. He just wants it. And Jezebel seems to get involved just to show the king's power—to prove that they can take anything they want. It's disgusting behavior. It's evil. It's straight out of today's headlines. So, when the prophet Elijah shows up and speaks truth to power, we all cheer, "Hooray! The evil king is going to finally get what's coming to him." Elijah starts in on a scathing judgment. He says "Ahab, because you did this to Naboth, God's going to punish you. The dogs are going to lick up your blood on this very ground that you stole—just like they cleaned up after

Naboth's body. And Jezebel too—she's going down. Thus, says the Lord." To this we say "Yes!" This feels right, this feels good, this sounds like Justice, doesn't it? And yet. And yet in the end it doesn't happen. There is no justice.

Instead Ahab puts on sackcloth and ashes, a traditional sign of humility and repentance, and God decides to go easy on him—which is typical of this prodigal God we worship. God says, "because Ahab has humbled himself, I won't bring punishment during his lifetime, instead I'll wait and bring vengeance on his descendants." So, nothing happens to Ahab and Jezebel.

Isn't that terrible? I mean, what about Naboth? Ahab didn't even try to give back the vineyard or make amends. And punishing Ahab's descendants for something he did—where's the justice in that? It really is a disturbing story. You've got your wolves, and you've got your sheep, and the sheep gets killed, and the wolves just seem to get away with it. No wonder we avoid reading this story—that's not the kind of lesson you want little Jimmy to learn in Sunday School.

But then there's another reason we North American Christians tend to conveniently forget this story. If we were to identify with one side or the other—who do you think we'd be? The poor guy who got killed because he wouldn't sell his land, or the rich people who got away with it? Are we the sheep, or are we the wolves?

Yeah. You probably see where I'm going with this. It's indigenous peoples' month. This Thursday is a national holiday celebrating the survival of the first European colonies on this continent. We all know what happened next. Many of us probably have reasons to disassociate with this history—to claim that it's not our history. But unless you identify as an indigenous person, we who occupy this land are less like Naboth and more like the descendants of Ahab and Jezebel—the people who God said would someday pay for the theft of the land and the murder of its inhabitants. Even if we're not directly descended from them, we have benefited from their crimes—that's the reality of our situation in Seattle. So, Happy Thanksgiving!

I know this is uncomfortable, but as Christians, as people who know that God is not okay with this kind of situation, what it is it we're supposed to be thankful for this week? How can we be thankful that Naboth was killed? My sense is that we're meant to be thankful that we're here, that we survived, that we have each other. But doesn't that kind of ignore the fact that our country did terrible things to get us here—that we're essentially descended from wolves?

I notice that the only redeeming part of this story of Naboth's Vineyard is the part where King Ahab laments a little bit after he's rebuked by the prophet Elijah. It's not a particularly impressive repentance—it seems rather half-hearted, but it's something. At least it gets God to keep from wiping him out. So, I wonder if that might be a more appropriate response for us this week of Thanksgiving. Instead of celebrating the abundance of this garden that was taken, we could maybe face the truth of its history, and express some remorse about turning much of the vineyard into a parking lot. We could ask for God's mercy, so that God won't wipe us descendants out--we could even try to discern what we could do to make amends—with the descendants of Naboth, with the land itself.

In so many of these stories that seems to be the hope: That it's not over yet. OUR story hasn't been finished. And we can make a change. We can choose to remember and retell the stories of those whose land and lives were taken from them. We can seek out the descendants of those peoples and try to make restitution and seek reconciliation. We can even learn to become more like them. More like sheep, less like wolves. To say to those Indigenous peoples who are still with us, "your way of life—your connection to the land has been more just, godlier than ours, so will you teach us? Will you please show us the way?" Now THAT would be a Thanksgiving celebration, don't you think?

I was thinking about Jesus. Jesus who was a descendant of this same kingdom and culture of Naboth and Ahab and Elijah—the people of Israel. Jesus was aware of this history—both about the Vineyard, and about the genocide of the Canaanites long before. Jesus knew his people had slaughtered others to take possession of the promised land. He knew his people were guilty. And instead of denying that guilt or running from it, Jesus took it upon himself—willingly, intentionally. Though Jesus himself was sinless, he took on the sins of his forebearers. As the son of God, he could have claimed a higher moral ground, but instead he humbled himself, taking the form of a servant, an agent of reconciliation.

I remember this one time there was a Canaanite woman who came to Jesus for help and Jesus wasn't sure what he should do—since, you know, he was a part of the conquering people, and she was descended from the dispossessed. This indigenous woman said to Jesus, "Hey I know you Israelites think we're dogs, but even dogs get table scraps, so throw me a bone here!" and Jesus said to her, "Well when you put it that way, of course I can help." The Son of God learned something about humility from an indigenous woman—can you believe that? I like to think the interaction was intentional. I believe Jesus was lifting this woman's knowledge, her intellect—

just as he often lifted Samaritans and Syrians as people to emulated. Jesus not only gave other people healing, he gave them dignity, even while learning from them how to live a more righteous life himself. That's the ministry of reconciliation for you.

On Wednesday night I was at a salmon dinner at my younger son's school where a member of the Duwamish Tribe shared a bit about his culture. I was excited to hear from him in part because of this story about Naboth. How blessed we are to still have guides in this area who are descended of the original human stewards of this land. Naboth has descendants today! Well this Duwamish man, Blake Shelafoe, introduced himself first in his native language and then explained that Blake is his taxpayer name, which made everyone chuckle a little. One of the things he taught the assembly was how in his culture, to express appreciation, Duwamish people don't clap, so much as they "lift one another up" with this gesture. This, he said, is in imitation of the cedar trees that are so important to the land. The top branches, he explained, are always pointed up to the sky in praise of the Creator. As the tree gets older, the larger, heavier branches fall lower, but they still help lift the rest of the tree. So, it is that the younger members of the tribe may reach the highest, but they still stand on the limbs of the elders. And so, we all participate in lifting one another up. Isn't that beautiful? Isn't that a great image for community? I wanted to hear more from this Duwamish man—not for the sake of his culture, but for mine. It made me want to support the preservation and sharing of this beautiful culture of his—for the sake of all God's people. So that we might lift one another up.

A couple years ago I was at a racial justice training, where the presenter, Heather Hackman, was talking about the importance of reparations in the process of reconciliation. Then last summer at our inter-community retreat, Pastor Cristian from Colombia said something similar. To get to reconciliation, there are three preconditions, he said: 1. Truth 2. Forgiveness 3. Reparations. You need all three, including reparations. Well Heather Hackman explained that for her reparations to indigenous people now includes paying voluntary taxes to her local tribe in Minnesota. She sends them a check every month as rent for the land that was taken from them by generations past. It's surely not enough to make up for what was taken but imagine if everyone did that. Imagine what a different experience Native Americans would have today if tribes across Turtle Island were paid taxes by those who live here.

Well lucky us, I discovered that on Indigenous People's day this year someone launched a website called Real Rent Duwamish that allows people in Seattle to pay voluntary taxes to the Duwamish Tribe—so that we can do this here in Seattle as well. Real Rent Duwamish. It's an opportunity I'm grateful for this week. I won't be able to give much, but at least now I know how to give something for the preservation of Duwamish culture. I've come to believe it's a form of reparations that is a necessary aspect of this ministry of reconciliation we've been given in Christ.

I was talking to someone about this after church last Sunday—paying taxes to the Duwamish Tribe-- and the question came up as to how legitimate is that tribal leadership—seeing as how they don't have federal recognition, and not all local indigenous people are on the same page, and how would we know that our money was going toward positive work—you know, fiduciary responsibility and all that. Reasonable questions. But then I thought about it and wondered, well how often do we know that our federal taxes go toward positive or just work? How legitimate is the leadership of the United States at this point? And yet we still pay federal taxes, right—whether we agree with our leadership or not? It seems to me that's part of this exercise of reparations—turning over resources and responsibility, without strings, without oversight even, trusting the Duwamish People to do whatever they think is best. Simply because we owe it to them. You could think of it as an act of faith.

Again, consider Jesus. Jesus who seemed to intentionally give up control on a regular basis. He was someone who didn't cling to land or money or possessions. He told his disciples not to rely on those things—not to store up wealth where moth and rust destroy, or thieves break in and steal. He told people to give these things away instead. If someone asks you for something—he said--don't resist, give them more than what they ask for. That was Jesus' advice. Consider the lilies of the field, he said. The birds of the air. Jesus seemed to relate to creation the way indigenous peoples do, have you noticed that? Other people thought he was crazy, of course. Naïve even. There are two types of people, you see—there are sheep and there are wolves. Jesus was telling people to be sheep. And so, predictably, in the end he met the same fate as Naboth. Jesus went to the cross to be slain like a lamb by those who wanted to take his kingdom. He could have gotten out of it, but he chose not to. Jesus said, if those are my two choices—wolf or sheep, then I'm going to be a sheep.

Well friends, the good news is that that wasn't the end of Jesus' story. In Jesus' story, our story, the wolves didn't win. Instead, we lift the good news that the lamb of God took away the sins of the world. God raised Jesus up to show that the way of love is the better way to go. Jesus even paid the price for Naboth's vineyard so that no one else must die for the sins of their ancestors. Forgiveness is now available. Justice is once again a possibility.

And we have been set free. We too have been given another chance to live in harmony with the land and with our neighbors because of this lamb of God who was lifted. But Jesus also made it clear that there's no room in the Beloved Community for wolves. We still must choose, this day, which way we will go. In this new kingdom, the resurrected Christ is with us as the great shepherd, teaching us what it means to be reconciled as sheep-- like Naboth, like our indigenous neighbors. May we give thanks and praise this week that we have been set free to pursue this way into life, and life to its full. Amen?

Where is God?
The Book of Esther

Today's Old Testament scripture is summary of a short, lesser known book that doesn't get much air-time in Christian circles. I can think of a couple reasons for this: first because the plot highlights a couple of women during a very patriarchal culture, and second because the story nowhere explicitly mentions God, even during a very religious culture. And yet still the book of Esther is one 66 books in our biblical canon. Isn't that something? The bible isn't just about spirituality and it's not all about men. It's good to be reminded of this.

And this book is a really good read. The book of Esther is a story about oppression and reversals. It's about power and jealousy and courage and retribution. It's the stuff of everyday life--men and women. And the question it asks us, by its very presence in our Holy Book, is indeed: "Where is God in the midst of all of this?" "Where is God?" Do you ever ask yourself that about your own life? Where is God during our everyday trials and challenges and sometimes reversals? Where is God in our stories of oppression and power and retribution--in the global refugee crisis--in the many genocides of the 20th century--in the political drama of our country--in the degradation of the earth? In the conflicts in our families--does God even notice?

The book of Esther presents God's people living in somewhat of a secular age, not unlike our own. Ruled by a rather bumbling dictator who is easily manipulated and prone to violence. Unfortunately, we still see those from time-to-time too. The story has a great plot, as do our stories--I'll run through it quick for you:

One day the king of this land--King Ahasuerus--is drunk at a banquet and he decides to show off his trophy wife, Vashti, to all the men of his court. But Vashti refuses to come out of her chambers. She refuses the order of the king! And King Ahasuerus is TICKED. He talks it over with the other men in the court and decides that he must do something about this, otherwise wives everywhere would start disobeying their husbands and it would be mayhem. So, he decides to replace Queen Vashti with a new, younger model.

That's where Esther comes in, you see. Young, irresistibly beautiful, and secretly Jewish, Esther is added to King Ahasuerus's harem and she quickly becomes his new favorite wife--the new queen. And with her to the palace comes Mordecai, the uncle who raised her. Once inside the palace Mordecai soon uncovers a plot to assassinate the King, and so he becomes a regular member of the court. But he's also Jewish, which means that he doesn't follow all the king's laws, namely bowing down to the king's right-hand man, a man named Haman.

So now it's the evil Haman vs. Esther's uncle Mordecai. Haman is irate that Mordecai won't bow down to him, so he tricks King Ahasuerus into decreeing that all the Jews in the land should be put to death, Mordecai included. Which is fine with the King because he doesn't know that his favorite wife, Esther, is Jewish and he's somewhat of a reckless fool anyway.

But, of course, Mordecai goes to Queen Esther for help on behalf of their people who are about to be annihilated. And Esther says to her uncle, basically, "What am I going to do--I'm just a woman, if I try to speak up, I will be killed." And Mordecai says to her, "Don't think you'll be safe just because you are in the palace--keeping silent won't help anybody." And then Mordecai has the famous line--"Perhaps, Esther," he says, "Perhaps you've been put in this position for such a time as this!"

So, Esther indeed does risk going to the King, and being wise where the King is foolish, she first points out that her uncle Mordecai had saved the King from assassination once upon a time--and he's a Jew. And then she outs herself as a Jew and uncovers Haman's plot to kill all the Jews. And the King is horrified and commands that the evil Haman be executed on the spot. Uncle Mordecai is given Haman's old job as second-in-command. Jews across the land take bloody vengeance on their enemies. And Mordecai's first order of business is declaring the occasion a national holiday--the festival of Purim, which is celebrated by Jewish people to this day. All because Esther intervened. Hooray! Justice prevails! Great story, right?

It is indeed an excellent story! Power to the oppressed! Speak up for those who are threatened! Use your power for good! And yet, again, where is God in this story? Where is God? Was God in the vengeance that Mordecai and Esther took on their enemies? Did God smile as Haman's 10 children were also put to death? Or as Esther asked for an additional day to round up all the enemies of the Jews? Interestingly, after everything had been reversed-- once Mordecai had taken Haman's place and the Jewish people were at the top of the social structure instead of the bottom, the story goes that all the people of the kingdom feared the Jews because of what Esther had done. It doesn't say that they all feared God or decided to worship the God of the Jews like Mordecai did. They just feared Mordecai instead of Haman. This wasn't a game changer, it was just a shuffling of the deck! The players may have changed, but the game remained the same. Because of Esther, the Jews were back on top, but what happened in the next chapter of the story? Did

Esther's actions mean the end of genocide? After Haman had been hanged, did they say, "Never again!"? Unfortunately, they didn't, did they? We know that this wasn't the last attempted genocide of God's people. And strangely enough these events didn't end the reign of patriarchy either. Go figure.

It's enough to make you wonder if there is any point to it all--if God even cared about this cycle of the story. And yet overall at least the people of God lived to witness another day. And at least two women in this story found their voices, right? So often we want our stories to feel like they have eternal significance--like we are changing the world with our daily actions or inactions and that nothing will ever be the same because of our witness. But the reality check of this story is that it doesn't really work that way. Not for us. We are every bit as flawed and fallible as Esther and Mordecai and Haman and even Ahasuerus. Sometimes we're up and sometimes we're down. Sometimes we are victorious and other times our stories may feel devoid of meaning--just a repeat of struggle after struggle, a daily grind that doesn't seem like it makes any real difference. God feels absent.

And the thing that even this scripture reminds us, by its lack of a redemptive storyline--is that only God really has the power to change the world as we know it. Only Jesus was given the power to redeem and to save us once and for all. Only he had the strength to forgive, rather than to perpetuate violence. Only he knew with perfect certainty when to be silent and when to speak. Only Jesus could choose to give up his life rather than save it, knowing that this was the reversal our world really and truly needed. And Jesus was able to do this because he was one with God--because he had the faith to rely fully on God's power and purposes rather than his own. Where was God in the story of Jesus? God was right here, in us. Not way up there, too high to be reached. Not down there--so small as not to be noticed. Not out of sight, hidden in a private room somewhere. Not even stuck in scripture, in the stories of long ago, or in trapped inside the walls of this church building. No, for Jesus, God was and is always here--in us. The very center of every thought and action. Our greatest longing and hope and fulfillment and truth. Where is God for us as his followers? God is here!

Can you imagine what a different history might have been written if Queen Esther and her Uncle Mordecai had felt this? What would the end of their story have looked like if Jesus had been with them as we know Jesus is with us? If God had indeed been the center of their story as well?

We also live in a secular culture, friends, as Esther and Mordecai did. And I wonder if perhaps their story is in scripture for just such a time as this! So that when violence and destruction threaten, we would find our voices as people of a different way--people of Jesus' way where God is abundantly present and working to make a change--sometimes with us and sometimes despite us. God is at work to bring mercy and forgiveness and hope.

And one thing we can affirm from this story is how good it is to celebrate when people are saved. When God's will is done. When God uses us to help someone in need. We do well to rejoice that God is working to make a change. Because we believe that God is here, and God is working--it's not all up to us! And so even if our actions big and small don't have grand or permanent consequences, they still mean something--because God is at work in the world.

We can rejoice, for instance, that the owner of Chobani Yogurt is giving a large portion of his fortune to helping refugees from Syria. Did you hear about that? . . . I heard him interviewed on NPR. Chobani *CEO* Hamdi Ulukaya said he knows what is like to be a refugee because he himself was a refugee when he was young--a Kurdish refugee who fled war with nothing and is now the head of a multinational corporation. When he recently visited a Syrian refugee camp, he said to himself--maybe I was put in my position for such a time as this--so that I would have the resources to help. For him that means over half of his wealth--around 2 million dollars' worth. I wondered if he was Christian--this man--since a lot of ethnic Kurds are Christians, he could very well be, but he never said, and didn't need to say. We can rejoice that God can work through anybody--Christian or Muslim, or atheist--it is simply good news to hear that God is at work.

I heard another story the same day about a young woman in our country--I'll call her rose. When Rose was about 12 years old, her parents picked up and moved to Mexico, and left her alone with her older brother. It turned out they were undocumented and under threat of deportation. The parents chose to leave their children alone here in America, where they figured they would get a better life. Rose didn't tell anyone where her parents had gone. Her brother quit school to work for rent and food. She tried to keep up with her own studies and make it through high school, but she found herself getting depressed and anxious. It wasn't until several years after her parents had left that Rose finally broke down and told a friend what had happened. And this friend of hers immediately reached out to help. "You can come to me for anything" she said "Books, rent--whatever you need." Maybe that was the whole reason those two girls became friends. For such a time as this!"

You see, we never know when we're going to be able to help someone in need. Sometimes we have obvious opportunities to be heroic--like when the late Daisy Dawson headed out to Japan following world war II. We will have a chance to hear about her redemptive work after our worship service. There are times when we too can say, "Here I am, Lord, send me!"

But you know most of the time people don't even know when they have had a significant impact on someone else's life. It could be that you smiled at someone or were kind to them when they really needed it. It could be that you were the example that gave your neighbor hope, or the stabile presence that helped a family member make it through.

Sue Rush told us a story at Session last week, about one of her sons, Mike, who when graduating High School decided to go around to thank all his teachers for helping him with his studies. He listed off to his parents all the people he was going to thank, but Sue and Jim pointed out that he had missed somebody. "Remember your 9th grade science teacher" they said--"the one you never thought much of? Remember how at one point in the year he kicked you out of class and told you to go study in the library for the rest of the semester because you should have been in a more advanced placement? Remember how the following year you did get into a better class, and how from that point on you tried to challenge yourself more?" "Oh yeah" he said. I guess that guy really helped me." Mike thanked that teacher, and the teacher was overcome with emotion and almost cried. He had never been thanked by a senior before.

After hearing that story, I found myself wondering about that teacher--the one the students don't think is very good. The one who sometimes wonders if he's ever making a difference. I wonder if he was in the classroom for such a time as that--to make a small difference in a young student's life.

And then I wonder about us too--we who ask sometimes whether our lives really make a difference, I wonder what moments God is planning for us-- moments of quiet faithfulness that can make a world of difference in the Beloved Community. Isn't it amazing how God crafts our world in ways that we sometimes can scarcely recognize, let alone acknowledge? What a gift it is--the way God is always working with us and within us--especially those who follow Jesus' way of redemption. Even when it seems like we are doing nothing religious--even when all we are trying to do is get by, still we know God is at work. It may be that out of our whole lives, only one day will be spent making a significant contribution to God's Kingdom. And yet even that is worth celebrating, and worth living for. May we all have these opportunities to Glorify God, friends, during our daily struggles--and as we celebrate these moments--may we find that our whole lives become acts of worship and provision and praise.

Spiritual Gifts
Isaiah 62:1-5; 1 Corinthians 12:1-11

What is your gift? What is your gift? In 1st Corinthians 12 Paul talks about spiritual gifts. He wants to make sure his people aren't putting each other down because they have different gifts. Some people are speakers of wisdom—they are wise. Some people are knowledgeable, he says. They have a lot of information. Other people are mighty in faith! Do you know people who don't have knowledge or wisdom, but they have faith?! There are other gifts too. Gifts like healing—people who heal aren't always doctors. Other people can work miracles too—sometimes those people ARE doctors, sometimes not. Other people speak prophecy, which means telling God's truth—often to powerful people or institutions. What's your gift? Paul's list continues. We could have the gift of discernment—the ability to recognize God's will. We could be people who speak in different tongues—the gift of communication! Maybe that means we can be understood in different contexts or different languages. That's a gift. Paul says the interpretation of tongues is a different gift—we might call it the gift of listening! Do you know anybody who has the gift of communication, but not the gift of listening? So again, I say to you, "What's your gift?" Do you have it yet? Turn to your neighbor, say "What's your gift?" There aren't many of us here today—you may have to shout for your neighbor to hear you, but that's okay, you go right ahead and shout, because not everybody has the gift of listening. Say to your neighbor "???"

That's a good question to get to the bottom of, because everyone has a gift, and when you don't know yours, you're less likely to be using it. Oftentimes it doesn't even matter what your gift is. Or whether you have correctly identified yours. After-all, as Paul reminds us—it is the same Spirit that creates these gifts, who gives them to us, who activates them. It is the Holy Spirit itself that is our gift. This Spirit simply manifests in different ways.

It's up to us to make use of the Spirit—or better yet, to let God make use of us!

I spoke last week about a time in the history of the people of Israel, when they didn't feel like they had this gift—or any gifts really. The city of Jerusalem had been sacked by the Babylonians, the nation's leaders had been taken as captives to Babylon. It had been many, many years since God's judgement upon the people. Instead of being The Chosen People, servants of the Living God, the Israelites had become the conquered people, the abandoned people, servants of their masters the Babylonians. And can you imagine what those demoralized captives probably heard daily? As they dug ditches and carried water jars and cleaned latrines in a foreign land, far from home? What they heard from the society around them was: You have no gifts. You are worthless. Useless. Expendable. You have nothing to contribute to society. Your lives don't matter. You are nothing.

How long do you think it took before the Israelites started to believe what they were hearing? They may have come into that city with their heads held high, but how long before their spirits were broken, and they found themselves shuffling along, just trying to get by. The prophets cried out on behalf of the people, saying to God, "How long, O Lord! How long must we endure these insults, these lies? We are the laughing stock of the nations. Your name is desecrated. Your people have become a joke!"

It's during this era of lament that one day a messenger is spotted at the gates. He comes carrying a scroll. He makes his way across crowded streets, through narrow passageways, past a vacant doorway, up some back stairs to meet a small gathering of slaves, tightly packed into a small bedroom. They have come to talk and to pray, and to keep alive that flame that still burns quietly within them. The messenger unrolls the scroll and begins to read:

¹For Zion's sake I will not keep silent, (says the Lord)
and for Jerusalem's sake I will not rest,
until her vindication shines out like the dawn,
and her salvation like a burning torch.
²The nations shall see your vindication,
and all the kings your glory;
and you shall be called by a new name
that the mouth of the LORD will give.
³You shall be a crown of beauty in the hand of the LORD,
and a royal diadem in the hand of your God.
⁴You shall no more be termed Forsaken,
and your land shall no more be termed Desolate;
for the LORD delights in you,
and your land shall be redeemed.
so, shall your God rejoice over you.

When the reading is finished there is silence in the room. But their hearts are strangely warmed within them. There are smiles on their faces, some bear tears of joy. And one by one they leave, once again with their heads held high. Saying to themselves, "Today I am somebody. I am going somewhere. I have been redeemed!"

As you may remember, God held to this promise. Just like God had delivered the people from slavery in Egypt, they also were delivered from Babylon, and later Jesus was sent to save all people from bondage once and for all—to give us all new names, to bless every child of God with the Holy Spirit, to say to every one of us "you are precious in my sight." But sadly, not everybody got the message. Even today, some people still haven't heard it, others haven't believed it, and some other people simply haven't lived into this Word that has been given to us.

Which is why unfortunately these things seem to go in cycles—history repeating itself to a certain extent. Let me tell you about another time, not so long ago or far away, when again many people of God were held captive—forced to dig ditches, and carry bales of cotton, and clean bathrooms for people they had to call "sir" or at least "mister & missus." We know what those demoralized people heard daily—because some old folks can still remember. No matter what they achieved, no matter how much knowledge they had, or wisdom, or discernment. Even if they were incredible speakers or listeners or healers, the people in power told them the opposite. You have no gifts. You are worthless. Useless. Expendable Your lives don't matter. You are nothing.

You would have thought that these people would have given up on God. Given up on justice. Kept their heads down and just tried to get by. But things were different for them, you see—because of Jesus, this time things were a little different, because they already had this Word! And it kept the Spirit alive in them, that little light shining within them, speaking words of love to them, so that no matter what anybody said, they never lost sight of their incredible gifts!

So, one day, a group of leaders gets together and says we've got to do a march. It's time to get together in the Capitol and make our voices heard. So, they put the word out. . . Gather on the National Mall on August 28th. We'll let the politicians know that we want jobs and freedom. We have gifts to use and we want the freedom to exercise them!" The little group of leaders doesn't know how many people to expect. The march is on a Wednesday when most people will be at work and it's far from people's homes. What if no one comes? The event could easily be a flop—a waste of time. On the morning of the event things are quiet-- it's still not clear what's going to happen. But then little by little the people start to trickle in. They come by bus, they come by train. Some people with little means even walks in from nearby suburbs. After a while the trickle becomes a flood and suddenly there is a sea of people in front of the Lincoln Memorial, maybe the largest crowd there ever for a political rally. All those people there to stand up and be recognized as having value.

The speakers for the day are passionate, eloquent, but the crowd is largely quiet. Some of them are so far back that they can barely hear at all. Even when a famous young preacher from the south stands up to the podium, it's still not clear that he will be heard. The people lean in to absorb his familiar cadence. The preacher leans out to project his voice over the multitude. The people fan themselves in the hot sun and strain to listen.

It's an ordinary speech, the likes of which he has given dozens of times before. Most of the material is the same too. Many of the people have heard it all before. He looks down at his notes here and there, wondering if they will hear it this time, if what he is doing will make a difference. And suddenly, he hears a voice from behind him. A familiar voice, an urgent, encouraging voice, interrupting his speech. "Tell them about the dream, Martin, tell them about the dream" she says. He looks up from his notes and pauses for a moment. He forgets what he was talking about. But that's okay because then he remembers something more important. His friend's encouragement has helped him to remember his gift of proclamation. He's not just a public speaker--He's been given a message from God—the God who will not be silent, the God who will not rest until the people are vindicated! He has been given a vision to share, and he knows how to share it. "I have a Dream" he says to that crowd—now a quarter million strong. "I have a dream. . . Even though we face the difficulties of today and tomorrow, I still have a dream. I have a dream that one day this nation will rise, live out the true meaning of its creed: We hold these truths to be self-evident, that all men are created equal. . . I have a dream today!"

I'd like to say at this point that the crowd went wild. That with each description of this dream, the people's voices rose with his, to say, "this is our dream too!" or "We shall overcome" But no. After the March on Washington there was no great fanfare about this speech. At the time few people thought it was any better than any of the other speeches that Rev. King gave. And yet we all remember it now. We all know what that dream was all about now!

You see it took the gifts of many other people to bring this dream into the public consciousness. Not just the gifts of a great preacher, though this was part of it. What if Bayard Rustin had never organized that march, or if Mahalia Jackson, Martin's great encourager, had forgotten to use her gift of encouragement that day, or at other times in his life? For this word to be received, still there were thousands and thousands and thousands of others who had to exercise their gifts of mobility to get to the capitol that day. They had to use gifts of listening to hear the word that was shared. Afterward, there were reporters who used their gifts of writing to spread the word throughout the country. There were professors and students who read and studied Dr King's speech and spoke to its greatness. There were lawyers and activists and common laborers who exercised their gifts to bring forth this dream of freedom and equity. The Holy Spirit was during the people during the civil rights movement and in the years since.

And yet still, in some corners this voice has not been heard, this dream has not been realized. Even after all of that. Still too many of God's people are held captive, some in buildings of concrete and steel, others held by unjust structures of society—structures of racial and economic bias, and many more are held simply by the voices in their own heads. Voices that continue to say to them, "You are part of a conquered people, abandoned by God, good only for serving the powerful and privileged." These voices say "You are worthless, useless, expendable. Your lives don't matter, you are nothing."

Friends the Spirit of God has not been silenced. Still, today, the voice of God cries out. Still there is this same message for the people—a dream to bring forth an even greater crowd of witnesses than those who heard Rev. Dr King. But who will speak this message today? And who will carry it? Who will be the organizers and the encouragers and the writers and the activists and who will be a part of the crowd? Is it maybe your gift that is missing? Truly the Spirit of God is with the people—the Spirit of God is now with us. How will God use you, today, in the midst our story?

What is your gift?

Good Intentions
Amos 5

I want to start out by telling you about something embarrassing that happened to me a couple months ago. I began a new initiative about a year ago, in early 2014, to start a Seattle Site of a national program of the Presbyterian Church USA called the Young Adult Volunteers. It's a mission's type program like JVC or LVC or MVS if you know those opportunities, but this one is with the Presbyterian Church. I had participated in this program myself for a few years between college and seminary and recently I saw a need for it in our area, so last year I got together a bunch of the alumni that I know in the area and we put together an application to the national church for the creation of a local site where young adults would be placed in agencies and churches around Seattle while living together in community. The tagline for the YAV program as they call it now is "a year of service for a life-time of change." Good times.

Anyway--I was leading this group of seven alumni as board members in this application process last year, and it turned out to be a lot of work. We crafted a vision, lined up partner agencies and churches, outlined a budget, welcomed a couple national church representatives for a two-day site visit--all of this took about 10 months. The whole time, the national church office told us it was looking pretty good, they'd get back to us. But then they did get back to us in November to say that we didn't make the cut for 2015. Which was disappointing. And the reason they gave that was downright embarrassing. They said our board lacked diversity. Not diverse enough.

And the seven of us were like, "What? So, our board is all young white people with similar backgrounds--we don't live in the same neighborhood--we go to different churches, we don't even go to the same Starbucks!" No, of course we didn't say that. We're not quite that oblivious--we were mostly just sad because racial equity is something we think about as individuals all the time. Most of us seek to develop an intentionally anti-racist mind-set. Once our application was approved, branching out would have been number 1 on our agenda as a board, beginning with hiring a person of color as the coordinator for our new program.

But at the end of the day, these kinds of good intentions weren't enough for the people reviewing our application. Our good intentions weren't enough. Even though it struck us as kind of ironic that here was a denomination that is almost 93% white telling alumni of its predominantly white program that we aren't diverse enough to work with them. Still, I must be the first to admit that they were totally right to turn down our application--I figure this means progress for the national church--good for them! It's not enough to want or plan for shared leadership and power--we must live it. And there needs to be consequences when we don't. I'm grateful for this kind of rebuke, even though it's painful and certainly not a fun learning process.

Have you ever had a similar experience in your life? When maybe your good intentions weren't enough? Or when you felt a certain rebuke on behalf of your team or your organization? It can be a bit discouraging, a bit hard to take.

I continue to also feel sad and a bit guilty on behalf of all white churches in general when I re-read Martin Luther King Jr's letter from a Birmingham jail like I did again this week. These words struck me sounding particularly contemporary this year. King wrote,

"In the midst of blatant injustices inflicted upon the Negro, I have watched white churches stand on the sidelines and merely mouth pious irrelevancies and sanctimonious trivialities. During a mighty struggle to rid our nation of racial and economic injustice, I have heard so many ministers say, "Those are social issues which the gospel has nothing to do with." And I have watched so many churches commit themselves to a completely otherworldly religion which made a strange distinction between bodies and souls, the sacred and the secular."

I think this should be a little embarrassing, because it's still true. For every white minister who took to the streets in response to the deaths of Trayvon Martin, Michael Brown, and Erik Garner, there were many more who went on with business as usual, as if police accountability has nothing to do with the gospel.

This letter of Dr. King was written over fifty years ago, and yet it is still true today that 11am on Sundays is the most segregated hour of the week, in large part because churches continue to behave in the way he describes--as if racial injustice doesn't matter. And that's just the churches that are still in operation. Also, fifty years ago, Rev King wrote in this same letter, that

"the judgment of God is upon the church as never before. If the church of today does not recapture the sacrificial spirit of the early church, it will lose its authentic ring, forfeit the loyalty of millions, and be dismissed as an irrelevant social club with no meaning for the twentieth century. I meet young people every day whose disappointment with the church has risen to outright disgust."

Dr. King met young people like that in the 60s. Don't we still meet young people like that today? Unfortunately, Dr King's prediction has proved to be an accurate prophecy. There are more and more young people who are disgusted with the church in general--the Millennials being the least Christian of any American generation in recent history, largely because they have seen the church as irrelevant if not hypocritical when it comes to issues of race, class, and sexuality--issues of justice.

And the hardest part of this rejection of the church, is that it is a fair one. It is often a true assessment. And our scriptures suggest that it may even be shared by God! Dr. King didn't come to these conclusions on his own simply from social analysis, but his was a prophecy learned from scripture that seems to have been saying similar things for thousands of years.

One passage Rev. King came back to again and again in his struggle for civil rights was this section from the prophet Amos, where God is blasting the people of Israel for failing to make their witness match their heavenly devotion. The leaders of the northern kingdom of Israel had become wealthy at the expense of the poor. They had developed an elite class that reclined on ivory couches drinking fine wine and listing to music played on delicate harps while others in their care went hungry, often without basic shelter or clothing. The religious leaders of the time might have said to the prophet Amos who was himself a migrant worker from the southern Kingdom of Judah, they might have said. "Well, Amos, we're not responsible for the increasing gap between rich and poor. We teachers of the law can't worry about all the homeless people or the sex trafficking, or the disputes between our two nations. God will work all that out someday--we're just here to worship and to wait for the restoration of the kingdom. Even if things don't look good now, at least we'll understand it better by and by. Right, Amos?"

But Amos wasn't okay with that explanation. And God wasn't either. God then said to the people of Israel, words that were relevant thousands of years ago, 50 years ago, and still very much today: "Forget about your festivals and your assemblies. I'm not interested in the noise of your songs or the melody of your instruments. Instead let justice roll down like waters, and righteousness like an ever-flowing stream. That's what I want from you. Says the Lord."

Good intentions weren't enough then either. It's never been enough. As painful as it can be to hear, we know from our scriptures that it's not enough to simply want justice. It's not enough to long for racial equity. God wants to see evidence that we are working for change. As in repentance, reconciliation, restitution. It involves risk and sometimes rejection--especially in the church.

Jesus once said to us, if someone has something against you, leave your gift at the altar, go be reconciled to your neighbor, then come back and continue your worship. Well, I'm going to make it plain this morning by asking, we who are here today, have we been reconciled with all of our neighbors? Every last one? I'm not just preaching to my white brothers and sisters here today--the wonderful thing about scripture is that it speaks to all of us. I know from experience that people of color can be just as resistant to racial reconciliation on certain levels--like when it comes to worship styles for instance. When it comes down to it, the kingdom of God is problematic for everyone, Amen?

I went to an undoing institutional racism workshop in December--one here in the neighborhood that members of Madrona Grace used to be regularly involved with. I had been avoiding going to this workshop because I thought it was going to be discouraging, and honestly, it was. After hearing for two days about how the church has supported racism, and how all white people are racist, and all the institutions of our society are racist because they were established by white people, well I came away from this feeling a bit discouraged and dejected--especially after having just had this rejection from the national church as well on account of my board's diversity clue-less-ness.

But you know, sometimes you're also in a good place when you're feeling this kind of low. Because then at least you find yourself looking up. After leaving that discouraging workshop, I also experienced a moment in prayer where I realized that at least as a Christian I am not without hope. Because the biblical story doesn't end with Amos chapter 5, or with God's judgment of the church, or with anyone's judgment of us. The story we live by has many other chapters in which the people repent, and there is forgiveness. We read that while God's anger may last for a night, still worship does not end. The people are not abandoned. Still there is an opportunity for new life for all who seek to do justice and steadfast love. We serve a God who pledges to take us back again and again and again--to prosper and not to harm us, to give us a hope and a future. And because of Jesus, the end that we know includes a new creation in this place, with leaves for the healing of the nations. This is the story we live by--a story of hope-- especially when things don't seem to be going particularly well. We are never without hope because it is never too late for us.

My story also, and our story together, doesn't have to end with the way things are now. And therefore, God has brought us to this place, to remember and retell these stories alongside our stories. So that it would not be too late for us. So that we also would have an opportunity to change, and an opportunity to be reformed in community.

My faith calls me to remember and rejoice that the amazing thing about following Jesus isn't that we always get it right--that we always do perfect justice and righteousness--rather because of Jesus we get to try again, and we're more likely to do better the next time. There may be times when we feel discouraged or disgusted with others or with ourselves. We may feel weary or worn out, but still God never gives up on us. God continues to call us back again and again to this difficult and sometimes draining road to racial justice. And we don't have to be afraid to begin again, because we know that God is with us during this journey. We know this in part because of the rebuke we find in scripture and in community--because God loves us too much to let us continue in injustice. God wants more for us than good intentions--God will not rest until we are producing the fruit of right relationships and equity in judicial pronouncement. As the UCC is so wise to affirm--God is still speaking in us and through us and to us for the healing of the world! As the Presbyterians are fond of saying, we are continuing to be reformed according to the word of God and the movement of the Holy Spirit. God is not finished with us, friends! This is the good news. Even when we hear it as rejection--it is still good news.

Because Jesus can and will redeem, reconcile, and restore us. He can do for us what we cannot do for ourselves, if only we are willing to face up to our own challenges and admit that we too need healing. We may say it's too painful. We may say we're tired and weary. But Jesus says *si se puede*. We say the problem is too big and we are too few, God says "here I am with you."

This is the day in our church calendar when the lectionary has us reading about Jesus' calling of the 12 disciples, so I kept that as a second reading. I think it's apt to remember that there's never a better time to spread the word about Jesus than when we ourselves might be feeling exasperated with our present state--our state of mind--the state of the church--the state of the world. Sure, we've got problems in Fergusson and New York, France and Nigeria. Yes, there's still 9 people on death row in Washington State, and black and brown people are mass incarcerated across this nation--we know we've got serious problems to address. But we Christians like Martin Luther King Jr--we also know someone who knows how to deal with these problems. And he invites us to come and follow as he leads us in dealing with them, here, now, today. So, we welcome others to join in this work, saying "come and see." Come see what gives us hope--come meet the person who promises us new life. And Jesus says more directly, "Come and follow." "Follow me," says Jesus, "into the way of humility and self-emptying. Follow me into service and public witness, and self-sacrifice. It won't be easy--he says--you'll have to take a good hard look at yourself and make some changes, but as you do so know that God does not condemn you. No matter where you find yourself--how righteous you have or haven't been. God loves you with the kind of love that never gives up and never ends. The kind of love that hopes all things, believes all things, bears all things--the kind that will never give up until justice rolls over your life like waters--righteousness like an ever-flowing stream. Take heart, my friends. In the words of Dr King, "The arc of the universe is long, but bends toward justice."

Let Justice Roll Down
Amos 1-5

I want to talk a little bit about water today. Water. H_2O. The stuff of life. It makes up 60% of our bodies and even more of our food. We drink it, we bathe in it, we cook with it, we play in it. Without it we would die. And we're lucky here in Seattle because we're surrounded by it. We know all about water here, don't we? That's one of the reasons I moved to this area—I love how much water there is! It's in our lakes, our rivers, our beloved Puget Sound. It's what keeps our forests and our lawns green, and it ensures that we schlep around rain gear for about 10 months of the year. We Northwesterners love our water. So, when the Prophet Amos says "Let Justice Roll down like waters, righteousness like a perennial stream" we can picture it. We can get into that kind of imagery. From the waters of creation to the waters of the New Jerusalem. These are our waters. We may not have the river Jordan, but we have the Cedar River and the White River, the mighty Elwha—even the Colombia. Now there are some rivers. Our rivers. It makes me want to sing.

"I've got a river of life flowing out of me. Makes the lame to walk and the blind to see. Opens prison doors, sets the captive free. I've got a river of life flowing out of me."

And as the song suggests, justice goes together with water. Praise God that Seattle is not just a place of water, it's a place of justice, am I right? Those of us who are lucky enough to live in the bubble love to talk about justice. This is the city of the $15 minimum wage. We just elected an openly Lesbian mayor—and sexuality wasn't even an issue in the campaign. We're proud of the fact that we are a sanctuary city, welcoming immigrants and refugees and spending significantly more than other cities on alleviating homelessness. We're not afraid to try and tax the rich in our city. It might not work, but we'll try. We're not shy about our liberal politics in general because we believe in justice. We know what that's all about. So, when Amos says "Let justice roll down like waters" we figure we've got it in the bag. This prophet is preaching our sermon. We're right there with him! Preach, brother, preach!

But then Brother Amos keeps going. It turns out he's got more to say. And not everything he says is encouraging or congratulatory. Much of it could even make us uncomfortable. He says most of it before this famous verse. We're tipped off by the "but" that proceeds the justice and the waters. You may have noticed this. The famous verse popularized by Dr. Martin Luther King "Let justice flow down like waters" only comes after some scathing rebuke for the people of Israel—people like us who also thought of themselves as the people of justice and the people of the waters. The point of Amos' larger speech is to take his people to task for a litany of in-justices that they don't seem to be aware of.

Like the oppression of the poor: "They sell the righteous for silver, and the needy for a pair of sandals." He says. "they trample the head of the poor into the dust of the earth and push the afflicted out of the way." He says. Amos accuses the wealthy of taking the last of people's possessions—so they don't even have a blanket to stay warm at night. He complains about the complacency and self-indulgence of the ruling class, those who drink wine bought with fines imposed on others. Amos mentions sexual sins too: How "father and son take advantage of the same girl" so that God's holy name is profaned.

The rest of the book is a diatribe about how God is sick of this in-justice. God roars like a lion with outrage saying, "Because you trample on the poor and profit at their expense" God says, "I hate, I despise your festivals and I take no delight in your solemn assemblies" . . . "Take away from me the noise of your songs; I will not listen to the melody of your harps," says the Lord. "But. . . But instead let justice roll down like waters. And righteousness like an ever-flowing stream."

That certainly changes the tone of this quote a bit, doesn't it? Especially when we realize that this prophecy is descriptive of our context here today as well. Even in our progressive, justice-oriented Seattle bubble—we've still got our problems. Like the way we also seem to be pushing the poor and afflicted out of the way. You know—how it's becoming increasingly difficult for anyone not making six figures to live here. We may have chosen between two progressive women for mayor, but they were both millionaires! And both white! Most of the people who voted in last week's election will go home to drink wine bought with money earned in part by Amazon or Microsoft or Starbucks, while the other half are struggling just to get by. Something like 40 or 50 percent of the people who live in this city are paying more than half of their income on rent. And those who can't do that end up on the streets, where they get fined if they try to sleep in the wrong place, and they have no access to water, and the government can routinely come through and sweep away the last of their belongings, so that they might be left without even a blanket to stay warm at night. It's not that dissimilar to Amos' situation if you think about it. And the sexual sins are still an issue here too. It's not often reported that Seattle is a hub for the sexual exploitation and trafficking of women and girls. There's Harvey Weinstein and Kevin Spacey in Hollywood, and then we've got some abusers here too, don't we? "But Let Justice Roll Down Like Waters, Righteousness like a never-ending stream." Says the Lord.

So at least we've got our water here in Seattle to fall back on. Or do we? I've been getting to know my local watershed recently. It turns out I live next to one of only two perennial streams in Seattle that feed into lake Washington—I'm very proud of my watershed now. There's Thornton Creek in north Seattle, which is the biggest, but there's also Taylor Creek down in Rainier Beach, which had water flowing down from Skyway into the lake all through last summer's drought. I go running along that creek frequently, so I think often about where the water comes from and where it is going. I learned more last month about the history of that water. How this whole area I traverse now was once the ancestral grounds of the Duwamish people, who fished and foraged throughout lake Washington, and along the Black River and the Duwamish River into Puget Sound. But then about a 100 years ago White Settlers took final control of this watershed by digging a channel from Lake Washington into Puget Sound and changing the course of the Cedar River. This geo-engineering dropped the level of the lake by 7 feet and caused the connecting Black River to dry up, which completely disrupted the flow of Salmon through Duwamish Territory. With nowhere to fish, the Duwamish people were easier to push out of the land. The powerful simply swept them aside. This was the first wave of gentrification in our area. The Duwamish tribe still has no treaty rights with the Federal Government 100 years later. And what has become of their great water? The Duwamish river is now a super-fund site. One of the most polluted waterways in the nation. Salmon that attempt to spawn in Thornton Creek have only a 10% survival rate, and there's no possibility of salmon at all in my little stream at Taylor Creek because the water has been channeled underground, to make room for concrete roads and sewers and people who often have no idea where their water comes from, and even less about where it goes after they flush it down the toilet. Isn't that sad?

"But let justice roll down like waters. And righteousness like an ever-flowing stream."

I was talking to a neighbor of mine the other day who got some bad news about her house. Her sewer line broke and she's going to have to get it replaced to the tune of $12K. It made me grateful to have had a sewer scope done on my house before buying it. But my neighbor said she'd done this too when she moved in years ago, and at that point she'd seen just a small, slight hairline crack in the pipe—nothing she thought she'd need to worry about. She said to me "I guess that's just what happens after nine years of water flowing through it. A little crack becomes a big one." And you know, that gave me hope! Not that other people's sewers are going to break—that would be terrible. I would especially not wish that for people like my sweet neighbor who doesn't deserve to have her basement flooded with toilet water, which is how she found out about the crack. No, what intrigues me is the reminder that water has this resilient way about it. This persistent and often powerful ability to resist confinement and diversion and blockage. It always finds a way to keep on rolling, somehow. You see that? It's not what we want in our streets or our sewers because it leads to potholes and polluted yards, but when it comes to resisting injustice. When it comes to undoing the last century of environmental degradation and displacement. . .slowly, steadily, quietly. drop by drop. Like an ever-flowing stream. . . YES!!! Yes!

Have you ever noticed a stream-bed, hewn out of solid rock? The work of water gently making a way for itself day after day, year after year, century after century. Can you imagine God's justice like that? Can you picture the abundant rain we have here gently cleansing the land of its pollutants, washing away our control, our neglect, our dis-placement? What a promise!

50 years ago, the great prophet Martin Luther King Jr. took up this call from Amos to oppose the racism, militarism, and materialism of American society. And the civil rights movement of that century indeed got things rolling again. Dr. King said with Amos, "Let justice roll down like waters, righteousness like a mighty stream!" But he changed it a little bit. Maybe unintentionally. Rev. Dr. King was also parting the primordial waters of the Red Sea, leading his people through dangerous waters, and trusting God to bring down a mighty torrent to engulf those who stood in the way of justice. Sometimes indeed God makes it a mighty stream, a powerful stream. But that's not the stream of Amos. That's not the kind of justice God is calling for in this prophetic book.

Here God says let justice roll down like an ever-flowing stream. A stream that never ends, that never dries up, that never dies—like my resilient Taylor Creek. It just keeps on flowing—even out of an impoverished, neglected, polluted area. Despite climate change. Despite toxic runoff. Even though we clog it up with endless forms of micro-plastics that choke fish and suffocate plankton and destroy coral reefs. God's justice just keeps rolling with it— rolling through it toward redemption, towards repair. It doesn't often come like a flood of mighty water. It's not like Katrina or Harvey—not devastating in that way. It's not even the kind of flood that ends up in my poor neighbor's basement. Instead God's justice is like the single drop of water that sends ripples across the world. Soft enough not to harm your finger, but strong enough to eventually wear down a rock.

Despite the injustice we see today, there are also signs of this water all around us. Sometimes hidden underground, but still active beneath the surface. We see it in small actions that can eventually disrupt large systems. Like Indigenous peoples successfully standing in the way of coal terminals all along the Salish Sea. We see it in rain gardens being installed to reduce sewer overflows during storms. We see it in damns being removed and streams being daylighted throughout Cascadia. We see it in education. . .My son has already been on two fieldtrips to two different watersheds through his public school, which gives me hope that his generation is learning more about water than mine was. And did you hear the announcement from the EPA that efforts to protect and restore the health of Puget Sound are so far proving effective? They need more money, of course, but it's possible we'll succeed in saving that body of water, just as previous generations were successful in remediating Lake Washington after decades of abuse.

And you know what else gives me hope? It gives me hope the way the word of God is still flowing today. In Church. Despite the pollution it's sometimes gotten there as well. I see hope in street prophets who like Amos stand up and speak truth to power. I have hope that God's word is still active in our hearts and minds, tapping on us gently but persistently, just as the water continues to work its way through the soil. We may not always notice it—it doesn't always make a splash. But it's there, and it's faithful in its work. Jesus said to the woman at the well, "If you knew the gift of God and who it is that asks you for a drink, you would have asked him, and he would have given you living water." Well we too have access to the fountain, and we too can drink of that living water. We have been baptized into its quiet power to overcome the world, and it is still here, welling up within us as the fountain of life! You, and I, friends—we are in this stream together. We can tap into it at any time—this well of justice. We can learn to roll with it the way Jesus did—through death and beyond. We can find the courage to dive into justice with Jesus and to go with its flow. When we step out to walk on the waters with Jesus, he helps us to stand. We may not feel the effects of his water all at once, but over time, if we let it wear away at our rough edges, we too can become a channel for God's righteousness. There is no gate or damn that can stand in its way. There is no blockage that God's water cannot un-clog. There is no mud or pollution that can dilute our potency. For we belong to the great plumber. The great wave master. The one who promised to get us moving, to get our 60% water flowing again into the Beloved Community.

Praise God that we in this time and this place are surrounded by God's beautiful, abundant waters. "So, let justice roll down like water, righteousness like an ever-flowing stream."

Message for the Captives
Isaiah 61:1-11

We sure had some interesting weather this week, didn't we? High winds, lots of heavy rain, now sunny, relatively warm. Apparently, there was Pineapple express hitting the West Coast for a while there with all sorts of flooding and damage. I went to take out my garbage the other day and things in my yard were all in disarray--patio furniture blown over, branches down. My bins were okay, but I noticed elsewhere that a lot of garbage cans had been tumbled by the storm so that there was trash spewed all over sidewalks and up in trees and clogging sewer drains. What a mess! I started thinking about all the work it was going to take to clean all this up. Who's got time for chasing plastic bags down the street? Who wants to go around picking up soggy napkins and candy wrappers? What a pain!

And then I thought about how these weather events are further evidence of global climate change--how this week we had record high temperatures here in Seattle, which doesn't sound bad, to have 65 degrees in December and plenty of rainfall, but then that also means there are some places that are flooding, and hillsides are being destabilized, and storm sewers are polluting the waterways, and heat loving invasive species are choking out native plants and animals--all because we keep spewing greenhouse gases into the atmosphere. The world is in a dire state.

And the other day as I looked at all the trash, I got to feeling a little bit grumpy, thinking about these things. How most of us will be spending a great deal of time shopping for gifts this week as the storms go on elsewhere in the world, even though all this shopping will simply create more CO2 and more trash to get blown about by the severe storms we are helping to create. And then how even if we are bothered by this climate problem, we're too busy working on other issues that are just as important and urgent--like making sure that our criminal justice system is treating all people equally--making sure that black lives are valued so that there is no New Jim Crow through police intimidation and mass incarceration. Or maybe we're busy fighting the sex trafficking industry, the modern-day slavery that still rages globally and is particularly vibrant in the Puget Sound area. Or homelessness---global climate change probably isn't a pressing concern for people who are sleeping on the streets this winter, though they know better than anyone how terrible it can be to get caught in excessive rain. And then capital punishment--I doubt the 9 people on death row in Washington State are thinking about the loss of habitat for polar bears this winter, though I'm thinking the nine million dollars we spend in taxes each year to maintain the death penalty here could probably be better spent working on these some of the hundred other justice problems that I haven't even mentioned.

It's maddening, isn't it? And discouraging to think about all the work it will take to clean up this mess we're in, if it's even possible.

I just read a great book called *This Changes Everything* by Naomi Kline, a Canadian journalist who lays out the case for why Capitalism is killing the climate. Through five hundred pages she makes the case for how all these systems of injustice are connected, and how we're really going to have to work together as a human race if we have any hope for systemic change. As I read it, I wasn't necessarily convinced that Climate change is going to change everything about how we work together globally, but it was interesting to note some of the things that she, a very non-religious person thinks will be necessary to save the planet. She talks about things like the forgiveness of global and personal debts, the redistribution of wealth, policies that make sure all human beings are valued equally-- like poor people living on hillsides in the Philippines, first peoples in the arctic who subsist on fragile fisheries, tribal people living on the edges of deserts in Africa where clean water is scarce. In order for the climate to be stabilized, the world's most vulnerable people will have to be valued just as much as the people of privilege whose corporations are running rough-shod over human rights. For the planet to be saved, we would have to put people before profits, sustainability and compassion ahead of extractive wealth and capitalist competition. All this from a secular journalist, but to me it sounds a lot like the kingdom of God!

As I read this book, which is a bit down on religion in general, I kept thinking, man, I wish someone with some influence would really take up this call and make it happen--make a climate movement like the abolitionist movement of the 19th century or the civil rights movement of the 20th century. We need someone like Moses to come along and speak truth to the corporate powers of our day. Where is the Frederick Douglass and Sojourner Truths? Where are the Martin Luther Kings and the Rosa Parks type leaders? Oh Lord, that you would tear the heavens and come down! Send someone to save us, before it's too late.

And as I read the scripture this morning, it's a reminder to me that God has sent someone--even more than one someone, to do this very thing. For post-exilic Israel amidst the desolation of the temple, that someone was embodied by the voice of Isaiah, saying, "God has anointed me, God has chosen me!" In the time of King Herod and the Roman Occupation it was Jesus who took up that call in his first sermon, reading from this scroll, this script, saying, It's me! "The Spirit of the Lord God is upon me, God has called me to bring good news to the oppressed, to bind up the brokenhearted, to proclaim liberty to the captives, and release to the prisoners, to proclaim the year of the lord's favor--the year of jubilee!"

This time of year we Christians remember how it was that when God came to earth in Jesus, he picked up this call from Isaiah to bring about the very reforms that we know are needed today--the canceling of debts, the redistribution of wealth, the end of the prison industrial complex, the end of modern-day slavery-- freedom for those in bondage, protection for the vulnerable, the return to a basic stewardship of the earth in which soil is built up rather than torn apart in search of oil or natural gas.

God sent Jesus to do this, to announce and usher in this re-ordering of our world--he called it the kingdom of God. That's what we celebrate at Christmas-time. That God loved the world so much that God came down to lead us into a better way of being in this place. In order to show us true justice and righteousness and stewardship and love. God didn't just look out at the brokenness of our world and shrug. God surveyed the damage we had brought upon ourselves and decided to get involved-- to come interrupt our severed relationships, our hidden addictions, our violence, our greed and hatred and fear. Christmas is about God having decided to get down and dirty with us, beginning with a messy birth in the filth of a stable, in order to identify with those others who are still refused a room at the inns of privilege-- children without health care, children born in refugee camps, children born to parents who have mental health challenges. God came down to start cleaning up our world, one substandard housing unit at a time. One polluted stream at a time. One corrupt institution at a time.

And the best part is that he invites us to help with this process--he invites us to get involved also. This too is part of Christmas. I mentioned last week how John the Baptist came to call us to repent and point to Jesus. Jesus is the center of what we do because Jesus embodied all that we are to be and do and change in this world, indeed Jesus came to save us. But the funny thing about Jesus is that though he was and is the only begotten son of God, he didn't just talk about himself, he also pointed beyond himself to all of us. John pointed to Jesus saying, "One is coming who will baptize you with the Holy Spirit and with fire--listen to him!" And then when Jesus had come and spoken, he then pointed to the Holy Spirit again, saying "With the Holy Spirit, you will do even greater things than I have done--even greater things."

And that's how the spirit is now truly upon us also. We who have been baptized into the life of Jesus, we are now the ones who can say, "The Spirit of the LORD God is upon me. He has anointed ME to proclaim the year of the Lord's favor." Following on these words of Isaiah, it will now be said of us, that WE will be called oaks of righteousness, the planting of the Lord. WE shall raise up the former devastations, repair the ruined cities, the devastations of many generations. We will do this--because Jesus has given his Spirit to all of us. Not just a few prophets like Isaiah or Dorothy Day or Oscar Romero, not just the super religious or the uber socially conscious or the well-spoken or the well-read. But all of us have this Spirit within us, upon us. And God will bring this good work to completion in us--this we have been promised! Because God is planting a new creation, and it begins with us! It begins this year, this Advent, this is the Day of the Lord, the year of Jubilee when all will be set right. This is our call from God and our mission as a people--WE are to lead the way into the new world order. Jesus will come to complete it, but we get to prepare the way.

And I don't know about you, but I find this to be good news. Because it gets me moving and gives me hope. We don't have to wait around for grand heroic leaders--the Spirit of God is already at work in and through us as ordinary followers of Jesus, and we have our marching orders--liberation, justice, the Beloved Community.

A couple weeks ago I got a text about a march and rally for Fergusson. It was a Tuesday and it was rainy and cold, and I didn't really want to go--I don't get all that excited about marches, to be honest--too often they can feel disorganized and ineffective. But I went out to this one anyway because I'd been invited, and I wanted to be supportive. I got there just in time on 23rd Avenue just north of Union where people were meeting up in a church parking lot, and since they were coming out of the lot just as I was getting there I ended up near the front of the small crowd. It was a decent showing, but nothing impressive, I figured I was doing my duty and started walking solemnly along with the others. But then I looked up and there coming from the other direction was another crowd, larger than the one I was in. As they got closer, I realized it was mostly young people--students from Garfield High School and when they intersected with our group and we all turned the corner on union headed toward downtown, the whole tone of the gathering changed. It was like a new spirit was upon the whole crowd--this mixed crowd of young and old. People were smiling and cheering, and there was energy in the chanting. Hands up--don't shoot! Hands up--Don't shoot! Black Lives matter! Black Lives matter! And then I remembered why I was really there--because the Spirit of the Lord God is also on me, as the Spirit was upon many others in the streets that day. Because the spirit of God is alive and active in our world, working towards the justice that we sometimes have a hard time seeing on the horizon. Sometimes you don't even know it's there, because it's coming from another direction entirely. But God is at work, and we get to join in that crowd--we get to join in with joy knowing that God has already begun to work it out, and yes, we shall see the goodness of the Lord in the Land of the living. Yes, we shall see the day of salvation, the vindication of our God, when justice will roll down like waters, righteousness like an ever-flowing stream and no further harm will come on all of God's holy mountain. When the earth itself will cry out with joy at the coming of the Lord of Glory, saying "Victory is mine, victory is mine, victory today is mine."

The other day I got a little sad thinking about all the trash and wreckage we must clean up in this world-- the devastations of many generations as Isaiah puts it--but you know it's amazing how quickly things get cleaned up when everyone pitches in. As far as I can tell all the physical trash is gone already-- from that storm at least. And God promises to be with us as we attempt to clean up some of our deeper global problems as well. Wouldn't it be amazing if we Christians helped lead the way toward the reforms that are needed in the world today? We have God's spirit calling us and empowering us to do this, so what more do we need? All we must do is pitch in and help--do our part in ushering in this new world order--the Beloved Community. We can even do it in different ways--some of us may march and protest, others may organize alternative Christmas fairs, some folks may just focus on loving their immediate neighbors. We all have a part to play. So, what's your part in the mission of God this year--in this new Christian year? How has God anointed you to proclaim the year of Jubilee? How will you join the mission of the newborn king, as he prepares to come again in glory? We point to Jesus, and then Jesus points to us. Saying "You get them something to eat." You speak truth to power. You get solar panels on your roof. Build. Plant. Redeem. And rejoice. Rejoice even during devastation. For surely, I am with you always, says Jesus. Even to the end of the world. Amen?

The Good Gift
Song of Songs

So... We get to talk about sex this morning! Whoo-hoo! If this makes you uncomfortable, you are certainly not alone--this topic makes pretty much everyone uncomfortable. And please don't worry about the children being present--I'm going to try to avoid the more explicit parts of the Song of Songs.

Just to be clear, this is the Old Testament *lectionary* text for this Sunday, which I've been preaching on all summer long--and other churches all around the world are talking about it today too. I didn't pick it specifically for the church picnic or to coincide with the blessing of animals. Sometimes these coincidences just happen. I was remembering for instance how last year on this day I ended up preaching about creation care and I casually suggested that it might not be a bad idea if we all ate a little less meat. Well that may have been poor timing given that we were on our way to eat an abundance of hotdogs and hamburgers. But that's the Lectionary for you, what can I say? Life is like that. If you wait for the ideal time to talk about something, it might never come. Carpe diem! Amen?

And it's especially like that with sexuality. Do you all remember having the sex talk with your parents or your children? Yeah. Not fun. Parents hate it. Kids hate it. Even couples don't really like Talking about their sex lives. And yet whether we talk about it or not, it's everywhere. Right? it's in advertising, it's in the news, it's in our gossip! You can't get away from it. Turn on the television and you're likely to get turned on yourself. Am I right? Even on public radio I'm amazed how often I must turn down the volume because there are children in the back seat. You know what I'm saying? Steamy stuff out there! Because sex sells. We are all hard-wired to find it captivating.

And sadly, the church has done kind of a lousy job talking about it in healthy ways. It's one of those hot-button topics that for some reason Christians shy away from addressing directly, along with money and power, and racism. And when we have talked about it, it's been mostly to point out its dangers. How sex can become an idol, how promiscuity can damage relationships and get out of control. Like with the ten commandments, we have tended to focus on the don'ts: Don't commit adultery. Don't have sex outside of marriage at all. Don't abuse sexuality through pornography. Don't become overly fixated on someone's appearance. Don't take the forbidden fruit. Don't even think about doing these things.

Lots of warnings and finger wagging. And to be fair, this is a lot of what we find in other parts of scripture--because the sad reality is that sexuality IS often abused in our world. Just like money and power--people have done a lot of horrible things with sex. But still--the scripture this morning suggests that doesn't mean that sex is bad. Just because sex is often abused doesn't mean that we should avoid sex or even avoid talking about it. Sex was first and foremost an aspect of God's very good creation, and as such we Christians should be able to celebrate it, as well as guard it. Because sex is good! Amen? Sex is good! When talking about Sexuality in the church I think it's important to keep in mind that the Song of Songs (or the Song of Solomon as it is sometimes translated) is one of 66 books of the bible, and its main distinction is the way it *celebrates* human sexuality! Even if it doesn't get preached on every 66 weeks, we're meant to remember that sex is a good gift to be celebrated.

I know there are other interpretations of this Old Testament book. Some early Christian theologians saw it as an allegory for the relationship between Christ and the church, or us and God. The male voice being God, and the female voice that I read this morning, representing us. Then the theme becomes the way in which we long for God and God longs for us, and that we are to experience communion with God. I can see the appeal for this way of reading the Song of Songs. But I also want to caution you against this interpretation for a few simple reasons.

One reason I question this approach is that God is not mentioned in the book. Israel is not really mentioned. Jesus and the church are certainly not part of the love poetry. So, there's one.

For another thing this metaphorical approach silences one of the few strong females voices we have in scripture--this is one of the only places where a woman speaks for herself and so making it all about Christ and the church robs us of that. Maybe this has made male clergy through the ages have felt better about reading "my Beloved is mine, and I am his" aloud in church, but it could be kind of a patriarchal rewrite of the actual text.

And then third, the spiritual interpretation encourages us to put off talking about sex with our children, even though they will continue to hear about it elsewhere. Besides, if it's all about Christ and the church, then phrases like "Open to me, my darling" are about going to church. Which I find a bit silly. Don't you? It's clearly the equivalent of a romance novel in antiquity. Any 12-year-old boy could recognize this book as a collection of sexualized love poetry. And Jewish people have pretty much always known this. In some conservative Jewish traditions, boys are prohibited from reading this saucy material until they are of an age when it hopefully won't drive them crazy with lust--preferably after they are married.

And yet is that really a good idea either--putting off reading love poetry until AFTER you are married? Hmmm.

What if instead we simply took this material for what it is at face value--a celebration of human sexuality that is meant to be a part of our regular practice of faith--central to the church community in which even little children are welcome.

For instance, a few of us were at a workshop last Sunday about children and racism. The main point of the presenters, which included a child psychologist, is that it is never too early to talk to kids about racial justice. Even though apparently kids don't start categorizing people racially until they are about five years old, they are still getting information on racial bias straight out of the womb, so it is our job to help them work out *anti*-racist attitudes as early as possible. Some people at the workshop wanted to push back a little, saying, "But we don't want to expose kids to all the hatred and abuse that goes on in the world--wouldn't that be damaging for little kids to have to deal with?" But their answer was, "No!" Even toddlers can understand when you explain to them that something is "unfair." So, the worst thing we can do is let them grow up in a world where injustice is happening and to say nothing about it. It turns out that silence is the only wrong answer--even poor attempts to talk about race are better than nothing at all.

Which, I think makes a lot of sense. It's our job to talk about race, even though it's extremely hard to talk about.

And if this is true, then shouldn't we also talk about sex from an early age too? Even if the main reaction from little kids is "eww." Wouldn't it be better for kids to hear about sex, and about the abuses of sex, from people who love them and care about their sexual wellbeing? And Scripture can help us with these conversations! Here's the beginning of that conversation from the Song of Songs: God created sex and it is good! Say that with me--"It is good!" It is good!

And here are a few other basic things we could say about sex, based on this beautiful collection of poetry.

1. Sex is good when it's between two people! Two is company, three is a crowd.

2. Sex is good when it is consensual--these two lovers clearly want each other--wow! This is not just the voice of a man, taking a woman, as was the case with David and Bathsheba--the section I read this morning was of the woman desiring the man. "Yes, means yes." Amen?

3. Sex is good when it's all about love. Does love to come first and then sex, or is sex an act of "love making?" Maybe it's a bit of both, but at its best sex is a consummation of love. It is love at its most passionate and intimate, the merging of two lovers in ways that are beautiful and a bit wacky.

4. Sex is good when there is commitment involved. I know it's not immediately obvious, but a closer reading of this book shows an interplay between desire and commitment. First the two people talk about how much they want each other, and then they talk about how committed they are to each other. Back and forth it goes. Sex can help sustain commitment, and studies show that it is most enjoyable when the participants are deeply committed to one another.

There're a few things already that hopefully we as Christians can affirm together about Sex. In addition to these simple truths, I also once heard this great image for sexual intimacy that I hope you'll find helpful in talking to others, since again, part of my point this morning is that we can and should be talking a bit more about sex with the people we love. There's no need to be embarrassed about it--God isn't! And so why shouldn't you be the person to talk to your niece or nephew or grandchild or god-children (with the parent or guardian's permission first, of course!). We have better resources to offer than HBO.

So, here's another image to consider: Think of healthy sexual intimacy as resting on a three-legged stool. The first leg is commitment. Without commitment, sex is cheap--a one-night stand, or worse it becomes exploitation. Free online porn, for example, is an extremely low level of commitment--all you might give in that transaction is access to your computer by hackers. This is not a healthy relationship. And by contrast, the highest form of commitment is lifelong fidelity, ideally in the covenant of marriage. Sex needs commitment to be healthy. That's the first leg of the stool.

The second leg of the stool is communication. Again, the yes-means-yes idea, but more than that--if you aren't talking to your lover very much, then sex becomes purely physical, and too easily manipulated into something else. Note how this biblical book--the Song of Songs--is a collection of poetry sent between lovers--it is an example of communication! This is what good sex looks like. Read the whole thing through and you might notice that they might never actually get around to the love making. It's all anticipation and desire here. At its best, sex can become the culmination of an intimate relationship in which no secrets are kept, verbally or otherwise, and this requires constant communication--maybe in the form of poetry.

Lastly, the third leg of the stool, is time. This may sound obvious, but it takes time to have great sex. Not just in terms of time spent in bed, but time spent in building a loving relationship. Even if you are deeply in love and committed to the person and talk with him or her all night--sex is not healthy if you just met the person yesterday afternoon. It takes an investment in time. I know a therapist who claims that sexual satisfaction can and should increase over the course of a marriage, to the point where only people who have been married forty or fifty years can experience what is known as electric sex--the absolute best of sexual experience. As a relatively young person I can't attest to this, but again, maybe we need to hear more from others in the community on this topic.

All I can say with certainty is that the three-legged stool of commitment, communication, and time is a solid foundation for healthy sexuality. What would be your thoughts on the subject? What would you say makes for good sex? It's a Godly question. A scriptural question! One that I hope you all will talk about when you go home. This is my charge for you today. That you would go home and celebrate the good gift of sex! Heed the words of the first reading this morning from James Chapter 1: Be doers of the word and not hearers only, Amen?

And this goes for you adults also who for whatever reason aren't in a committed relationship. Sexuality isn't all about the physical act of intercourse--the Song of Songs is more than that. So, I'm giving you my permission as your pastor to think sexy thoughts; feel sexy feelings; give thanks for sexy looking people; to praise God for sex. Remember the three-legged stool, be responsible, be loving. But praise God for Sex! If you don't have a partner to talk to about sex today, then at least get dressed up tonight and let yourself feel sexy. God made your body and it is good.

One more quick side-note for the aged among us. There's a lot of controversy about sex in nursing homes these days. Adult children of the elderly are scandalized by the idea that their parents are still sexually active in their geriatric years. Well why shouldn't people enjoy their bodies right up to the end? They're still good you know! Nowhere in scripture does it say that sex should be over for us decades before we die. I heard about a Jewish elder-care facility on the east coast where they encourage sexual activity. Safe sex, of course, but it's in the paperwork that they make families sign--that sex is a good activity that should be celebrated when it is consensual. This works because they are a Jewish facility. Their main frame of reference is the Hebrew Bible, including this very important book. One more reason to celebrate our Jewish heritage in Christ.

Now back to the instructions. If you do have a lover at home, I'm sure he or she will appreciate you dressing up and feeling sexy tonight too. Or better yet, why don't you get dressed down and feel sexy. In Jewish tradition it has long been considered a bonus to make love on the Sabbath--since the Sabbath is our celebration of the good gifts of creation, including love and sex. So maybe you could surprise your lover tonight wearing nothing but a bathrobe. Or if that would freak him or her out, maybe just make a conscious decision to slip into bed naked tonight and see what happens. Or at least send a love note, for goodness sake! Taking risks is part of sexuality too you, know. Risking disappointment is a good thing. Jesus didn't talk much about sex, but he did have a lot to say about taking risks. In this context that might mean putting yourself out there. "Don't hide your treasure!" Said Jesus! "Naked and unashamed," was the good creation of our Lord. Our God of love! So, let today's scripture be a reminder that God wants you to make use of what God gave you so that you can bring a return on that bodily investment of yours. And I'm not just talking about children. Children are great--babies are a wonderful gift too. But sex is for far more than just children. I'm talking about profits of joy, of love, of the glory that comes from being in full communion with another human being. This is part of the reason God gave us bodies, so that we would experience life and life to its full!

Anyway, you get the idea. Write a love poem. Read the Song of Songs by candle light. In the bath. Together. Tell a friend that he or she is sexy. A friend--not a stranger. And please talk to someone in your family about God's good gift of sexuality. Friends, the Glory of God is a human being fully alive, and the Godly life involves good sex. Amen? Amen!

The Wisdom of God
Proverbs 1: 20-33

Do you ever wonder where wisdom is when you need her? I sometimes do. Where is this beautiful sage our scriptures speak of when we are faced with decisions that could change our lives forever? Where do you find wisdom for making concrete decisions-- Like choosing where to live, or how get a better job, what to teach children, how to organize finances, or even just what to have for dinner? I can spend a ridiculous amount of time pouring over a simple restaurant menu, let alone a voting ballot! How does one ever feel wise enough to engaging in local or national politics? Life is too complex. Decisions are hard. They can have hard consequences. And sometimes it feels like there is little guidance on how to go about making them.

Of course, this isn't to say that there's a lack of advice out there. We all know people who are more than happy to tell us what we should do. Everywhere you look there are experts giving tips on how to fast-track your career, how to get out of debt fast, the 10 best foods to eat to cut that belly fat. It seems like everyone claims to be wise these days. We've got advice columns and life coaches and pushy family members with their own competing brands of wisdom. The problem today surely isn't a lack of information or options or advice. The challenge is discerning who to listen to--how do you decide what advice to take--how do you identify true wisdom--? We know she's in the crowd somewhere, but how do you find her when you really need her. Like when suddenly, your mom is on life support, or your marriage is on the rocks, or your boss calls and it's not good news. Where is wisdom when there is a global refugee crisis?

For us Christians, scripture seems like a good place to look. And I certainly believe that reading the bible regularly and carefully can build a good deal of wisdom in us over time. But the problem with the bible is that it's not really a how-to book. As much as we Christians sometimes try to package it as a step-by-step guide to faithful living, scripture is rarely quite that clear or direct. For one thing, there is sometimes conflicting advice in the bible just like there is everywhere else in our lives. Here in the book of Proverbs for example, which is mostly a collection of sayings worth pondering, there are verses suggesting that we should pursue wealth and celebrate it, and then there are others cautioning us about the dangers of money. Some of the proverbs suggest that righteousness will be rewarded, others say that the wicked will prosper. We can come away with some good overall guidance-- wisdom is good, foolishness is bad. But what exactly is wisdom again? How is it distinguished from foolishness?

And sometimes certain passages can even be a little discouraging. The one thing we could say from this chapter is that it would seem as though Wisdom is the one that laughs at us when we get it wrong. She is the 20/20 hindsight that shakes her head and says, "I told you so." In all fairness, she probably did warn us. Her voice was one of the ones in the crowd, and we just missed it somehow. At least that's been my experience. Most of the time when I look back at a foolish decision I made, I see how I should have known better. I should have seen that coming. But I didn't. And now wisdom is laughing at me. As the scripture says, it feels as though she mocks me when I am in a panic. And so, I wonder if it's my own fault that I can't find wisdom when I need it. Maybe I ignored her too long, and now she hides herself from me in punishment, because, again, as it says here in Proverbs, I hated knowledge and did not choose the fear of the Lord. And now she has given me over to deal with the mess I've made of my life.

It's a rather distressing concept, wouldn't you say--this image of God? It reminds me of that Proverb Jesus referred to in the gospels. "To those who have, more is given, and to those who don't have, even what they have is taken away from them." How sad if this is true of wisdom as it seems to be true of wealth. Because it means if we don't already have wisdom, then we are doomed to be fools for the rest of our lives.

And yet, does that sound like the God we have known in Christ Jesus? Is God someone who condemns us when we fail and then refuses to answer us when we try again? Sadly, I see a lot of people living with this god on a daily basis--folks who have a hard time getting up in the morning because it feels as though the universe is against them, and they have no hope of ever making a change. Why even try to be wise if you suspect that you will just come out looking like a fool again and again and again--if life is simply a matter of accumulating mistakes? I suppose if that was the case, we'd just try to cope as best we could. Life would be simply about survival, and little more.

But what I want to remind you of this morning, friends, is that this isn't the story for us. Or at least it doesn't have to be. God doesn't want it to be our story. We who have been baptized into the life, death, and resurrection of Christ Jesus--we are given a different story. Because in Jesus, God made it so that we don't have to accept that kind of defeat.

If you were here on the day of Pentecost this year, you may remember me referencing today's text from proverbs. Pointing out that Jesus was the embodiment of lady wisdom. And how wisdom was then given to us in the form of the Holy Spirit, so that now, today the Holy Spirit is with us. "She is with us indeed!" Remember? And we know that this Spirit of God is not against us, she is for us. She loves us with a perfect, unceasing, undying, never-giving-up kind of love. No matter what we have done or left undone, no matter how foolish we have been or may continue to be, still, she is with us. She is with us to encourage us, to guide us, to protect us, to comfort us, to build us up, to speak to us words of consolation and hope--and wisdom! This is not the wisdom of the world that simply tells us we reap what we sow. This is not the wisdom of the dominant culture that tells us might makes right because only the strongest will survive. This is a different kind of wisdom. It's the wisdom that uses so-called foolish people to shame the wise. It's the story that claims those who lose their lives are the ones who will find them. It's the wisdom that lifts the broken and downtrodden while bringing down those who are proud and arrogant. It's the wisdom of forgiveness and mercy and grace. This is our gospel--the story we celebrate and share. It's a story of hope!

So, let's look at this passage again, through this lens of Jesus, our Lord of mercy and grace who is and will always be the best interpreter of scripture-- our best and only hope of finding true wisdom.

The Holy Spirit reminds us that when Jesus told proverbs in the gospels, they often came out a bit differently than people expected. Like, "You have heard it said, "an eye for an eye, a tooth for a tooth," but I say to you love your enemies and do good to those who persecute you." This was a pretty big reversal at the time. Then there was "You have heard it said, thou shalt not murder" --there's a good proverb, a fairly basic command— "but I say to you that anyone who is angry with a brother or sister will be subject to judgment." Jesus goes on to say that anyone who calls a brother or sister a "fool" will be in danger of the fires of hell. So now the command for us is more like, don't be angry, and don't call people fools. I'm thinking of it as the Mr. T proverb. As in "Who you are calling a fool, fool?"

We should beware when we find ourselves passing judgment on the wisdom or foolishness of others. The passage from the book of James also reminds us of this today. We must be careful what we say--where our tongue s takes us. Don't call others foolish, and don't call yourself a fool, lest God's judgment burn against you! For you too are a child of God for whom Christ died. And Christ would never have you labeled this way. "Who is in a position to condemn?" Said Saint Paul--"Only Christ, and Christ died for us, Christ rose for us, Christ reigns in power for us, Christ prays for us!"

And Christ's Spirit is still with us, as lady wisdom was, crying out in the street, during our everyday routines. She is there with us, speaking to us through the common events of our work-a-day world, trying to rouse us from our dreary slumber of despair. "Pay attention." She says. As she tries to talk to us through our bosses and our spouses and sometimes even our pets. Wisdom is everywhere. And oh, that we would hear her! "I will pour out my words on you," says the Holy Spirit, "I will make my words known to you." She promises us. "Those who listen will be secure, without dread of disaster."

How will we know it's her? Friends, we recognize wisdom when she reminds us of Jesus! "My sheep know my voice," said the great shepherd, "I know them, and they know me." Which means that we already have God's wisdom--she is here with us, now. Where is she when things go down? She's here--on the cross. And here--at the table. And here--in our hearts. And here--in our minds. And here--where two or three are gathered together in Jesus' name.

She says that those who listen to her will be secure and will live at ease, without dread of disaster. May it be so for us, as we become slow to judge and quick to listen. May we also feel secure and at ease. This is the hope and promise from today's scripture.

But notice also what this passage does not say. Today's scripture doesn't say that we won't face disaster. Lady wisdom doesn't promise that we will live happily ever after. Just that we will be secure. As in not in-secure. As in not worried or anxious all the time. As in grounded. Sane. We can be comfortable making hard decisions because we know we won't be condemned when we make mistakes.

There is a psychiatrist named Viktor Frankl who survived the holocaust and has written extensively about his experience of disaster in a concentration camp. One of his learnings from that horrific experience was to affirm that in the end there is only one thing that no one can take away from you--your ability to control how you respond to what happens in your life. You can't always control what happens to you. Bad things do happen to good people, to faithful, wise people. And wise people also make mistakes. But how you react when bad things happen is up to you. No matter whose fault it is, we can choose to have hope and to offer grace. We can decide to try again. We can cultivate a growth mindset. We can live as though the end is not the end.

And you know who says this better than anybody? It's Jesus! The voice from heaven comes to us saying "listen to him." Listen to his voice--look for his wisdom. Spend time with him in prayer, in scripture, in worship and fellowship. Remember that those who seek first his kingdom and its righteousness, they are secure. Secure in the love that lifts us up and never lets us go. Confident that Christ's wisdom can and will cover our foolish mistakes. Joyful that we get to live and reign with him no matter how often we go astray. Because our good shepherd promises never to leave us or forsake us. "I know the plans I have for you," says our incarnate Lord, "plans to prosper and not to harm you, plans to give you a hope and a future--one that is safe and secure from all alarms." May we know that kind of wisdom, friends. May the God of hope fill *us* with all joy and peace in believing, so that by the power of the Holy Spirit *we may abound in hope* and so live as people of gratitude and grace.

Moving On
Ruth 3-4

There continues to be a lot in the news about the refugee crisis in Europe. Millions of people are still fleeing war-torn areas of the middle East seeking safety wherever they can, in boats, on trains, in over-crowded refugee camps, on the side of the road. Governments within and beyond Europe are arguing over how many people they are willing to take in, with politicians taking heat for promising too much or too little. I read that the prospect of taking in large numbers of Muslims has led to a crisis of identity in Germany in particular, where neo-Nazi groups are at odds with their government's very inclusive policy. Our hearts go out to the refugees and politicians alike, knowing that in this era of terrorism and international insecurity, there are no easy answers. And as people here consider how we might welcome refugees from Syria, we are aware that migrant challenges are nothing new to this country either. How do we balance the needs of Syrian refugees with the needs of the thousands of migrants from Latin America who travel to Washington state each year, or the large numbers of Somalian and Sudanese refugees who have made a home in Seattle, some of whom come for a while to live right here, downstairs at Julia's Place?

It turns out that these questions of ours, complicated as they may feel to us, are as old as the bible, and today's scripture is very much about this issue of migration and provision. The book of Ruth in general is THE quintessential biblical story of hospitality—written at a time when xenophobia was a hot topic for the people of Israel, provided as a sort of fable about how foreigners should be treated.

The story goes like this:

There's a woman named Naomi whose family is forced to flee their country on account of famine. They become refugees on account of food insecurity. This continues to happen today on account of drought. And Naomi's family has no choice but to seek refuge in the land of the Moabites, who were the religious enemies of her people. So, they are forced to live in enemy territory. That must be what it feels like today for extremist Muslims to seek refuge in Christian nations, wouldn't you say?

So, the first surprise in the story is that Naomi's family receives welcome in Moab, even though they are enemies—it's kind of like the story of the good Samaritan that way. Naomi's sons marry Moabite women, her family is provided for. Hooray! Only then tragedy strikes again. Suddenly all the men die off. Naomi's husband, her sons. Leaving her without anyone to go out and bring home the bacon, as was the only way to survive in the ancient near-east. Without men, women became destitute. This must have been really disturbing for Naomi—to have been saved from famine just to become widowed down the road. Imagine what it's like for refugee families in our nation today, who escape war and famine in their home countries, only to encounter prejudice and racial profiling in their new home. What happens to women whose husbands and sons are carted off to jail or deported? It must feel like insult to injury.

So, Naomi understandably feels rather deflated. She tells her two daughters-in-law, "I'm going back to my home country. If I'm going to be homeless, I'm more likely to find charity among my own people. You two girls are still young. I know you will find new husbands among your people here in Moab."

But then comes surprise #2. Not only has Naomi been welcomed by her enemies the Moabites, but then one of her Moabite daughters in law isn't willing to let her go back to Israel by herself. This woman named Ruth decides it is her obligation to care for Naomi no matter what, even if it means leaving her own country to assist her. She says to Naomi that famous line "Where you go, I will go. Where you stay, I will stay. Your people will be my people, your God will be my God." Some have described this as radical faithfulness, but you could also see it as an amazing act of hospitality. Ruth was unwilling to abandon this old woman she had welcomed into her life. Once Naomi was a part of Ruth's family, she would do whatever it took to care for her. Isn't that remarkable?

The rest of the story is then about what hospitality looked like on the other side of the border. How when they went to Israel, Naomi taught Ruth how to gather food according to the laws of God that provided for people like them who were destitute. And then she also knew there were laws concerning the care of distant relatives who were in need. Do we have people in our country who help immigrants and poor people understand our laws and receive help in times of need? Who are they? Can you shout out the name of an organization or two? Who does this work of hospitality professionally? How about the NW immigrant rights project? Tierra Nueva up in Burlington. Conejos. Mary's Place. I learned more this week about a group our church gave money to called Puentes—they do a lot of counseling with people at the immigrant detention center in Tacoma.

Well today's selection from the book of Ruth is a more personal example. Naomi instructs Ruth specifically here about how to get herself a husband. She explains the local customs around dating and courtship, which, given the details in this story, some instruction was clearly needed. I don't know of any organizations that do that kind of work in our culture. Do you? It takes a friend to give that kind of advice. And Naomi is already more than a friend to Ruth—she is family. Ruth had taken her in as family and now Naomi is taking her in—by setting her up with a relative of hers. A guy named Boaz, who was a so-called "kinsman redeemer"—someone obligated to help on account of distant family ties. I don't think most Americans have that kind of sense of obligation—where you could arrange a marriage based on need. But you know who does? It seems like people from Latin America have a strong sense of family. Familia! I wonder if we have something to learn from the people who come to pick our vegetables each summer.

Which brings me to surprise number 3 in this beautiful story. Lest we think that Boaz is really the savior of these two women. Something you should know about the hero in our soap-opera is that he may have been willing to marry a foreign, Moabite woman named Ruth (which was more than frowned upon in ancient Israel). Boaz was old, and he came from a questionable family—so he wasn't exactly a great catch himself. The thing that everybody knew about Boaz was that his family was descended from an incestuous union between a man named Judah and his widowed daughter-in-law (something that was also highly scandalous and frowned upon in ancient Israel). I know, it's complicated and hard to follow as family histories often are. But the point is that Boaz's family honor was just much in need of redemption as Ruth's was. And somehow the two of them getting together fixed all of that. One vulnerable person, welcoming another vulnerable person in all his and her hurt and fear and need. It was a beautiful union-- Two incomplete people producing one whole. In this case there was literally a child that came about because of this union, named Obed, which meant "Servant."

And the surprise ending is that Obed's grandson was King David—the most famous king in all of Israel's history. King David was descended from a foreign Moabite woman on one side and a disgraced child of incest on the other. I bet that really upset some people when they found out about that. It's like today when you point out the mixed ancestry of prominent Americans. How we were all immigrants once in need of hospitality, except maybe for some Native Americans or Chicanos, and a lot of Spanish speaking people have more claim on this land than we do. What would it be like if we were all able to point back to some ancestor who received hospitality in a time of need? Would that make us more likely to offer hospitality ourselves? What if, as Christians, we traced our most important ancestry through Jesus, who was a descendant of David, a product of Ruth and Boaz?

Oh, and don't forget about Naomi! Since this book is more about her redemption than it is about Ruth. In the end it's the old woman who is saved. Ruth might have been alright if she had stayed in Moab like Naomi's other daughter in law. She probably would have married a local boy, and all would have been well for her there too. But Naomi was the one who wouldn't have gotten very far without the help of this Moabite foreigner. She might have ended up dying poor and homeless, but instead Naomi was welcomed into the home of Boaz and blessed with a grandchild in her golden years. Indeed, at the end of the story it is Naomi who is blessed by her neighbors--they say, "A son has been born to Naomi—the Lord has saved HER!" All because of the foreign Moabite who embraced her.

Well wouldn't it be amazing if that was how elderly people in our culture viewed young immigrant women today—the ones who are having the babies that often their own children are not? Regarding the European refugee crisis, more than one scholar has noted that this may be exactly the boost in population that European countries need, now that their birth-rates have fallen below replacement levels. I read an article a few years ago about how the Italian culture is facing extinction on account of the lack of young people willing to have more than one child. Well suddenly they have more babies heading toward their shores than they can handle. Those babies may not have been born in Italy, but if they grow up to learn to cook Italian food, the world will rejoice. And the same thing is true here among white people by the way. The reason there will be no racial majority in the latter half of the 21st century is because of immigration. This is how God is providing for our economy. This is how God is giving us a hope and a future—through the gift of hospitality.

And that's what I hope you will remember as the main point of the book of Ruth as a whole: That providing hospitality is how we are provided for. It is in hospitality that we ourselves are welcomed into God's Beloved Community. Those of you who have lived this, in more than just theory, you already know that this is true. As you have welcomed children and neighbors and co-workers into your lives and found that you received more blessing than you ever gave. How when you reach out in welcome, you find that you are welcomed into a new culture, into a new perspective, into a new appreciation for God's incredible love. I'm not saying it's easy. Sometimes what hospitality does is simply break our hearts, so they can be put back together in new ways. But in the end, you'd do it all over again, wouldn't you? Because somehow that experience made you a better person?

In our life together as a community, we also affirm that it is in welcoming that we are welcomed, it is in providing hospitality that we are provided for.

The other day I was reflecting on my hopes and dreams for this congregation. One of which has been that the neighborhood would know us and value us. I always thought that would happen because of some new or innovating program we might have for the immediate neighborhood—like how we used to have a community center in the 60s or the tutoring program that was here in the 80s and 90s. But now when I meet people in the community, you know what they say to me? "Oh, you're the church that does Julia's Place—it is so wonderful what you have done there, thank you so much for providing for those families." And I think to myself, shoot, we haven't done all that much. Sure, we renovated and gave over the basement, but Mary's Place runs the operation now. If anything, they are the ones providing for us—giving us a hope and a purpose. All because we simply said yes to some neighbors in need. It has been in welcoming others that we have been welcomed into a new community.

And the same is true of welcoming Liberation UCC. I don't think many of you were able to go to their Seven Last Words service last spring, but wow—what a gift it is to have so many amazingly gifted preachers and teachers and musicians among us on a weekly basis. I continue to make new connections through that fellowship all the time. They have welcomed us into the joy of their "network of affirming ministries" and it is a joy. What I thank God for most of all is how this has opened us up to new forms of hospitality. There have been over a dozen different groups that have used the Madrona Commons since we launched last spring. These groups have donated to help maintain the space, and they have spread the word so that we've rented out an office and are in conversations with a Jewish Synagogue that may be interested in sharing space with us as well. By the end of this year we may be at a point where I can say that another of my long-standing prayers for Madrona-Grace has been answered—that the building would pay for itself. It's almost true! Because of hospitality. Because when we look to provide welcome to others, we ourselves end up being the ones who are blessed.

And when we are blessed, then we have more to give to others, because we are blessed to be a blessing—to produce Obeds—servants. So, what's next for us? Well what if we were like Ruth and imitated her sense of hospitality. It wasn't enough for Ruth to welcome Naomi into her house. When Naomi was in need, she also then went out, away from her space of comfort and provision, in order to care for this person God had put in her care. So, what would it look like for us to go out? To extend our hospitality and service beyond this place of sanctuary? Can we trust and believe that God will be with us, will continue to provide for us as we seek to provide for others?

There is no shortage of opportunities to do this, friends. Maybe it will mean welcoming strangers into our homes the way we seek to welcome them in the church. Maybe it will mean advocacy for those who are kept from us because they have been priced out of the neighborhood, or locked up in an immigrant detention center, or must take a bus to a tent city out near North Bend. Maybe hospitality means going to see them! Or maybe it means simply accompanying the people God has already placed in our path—like the folks downstairs who probably already have friends in these distant places.

May we be like Naomi, friends—people who graft others into our families, knowing that our redemption lies in how well we practice hospitality. And may we be like Ruth—willing to go the extra mile for those whom God has given us to love.

For we know that truly it is in providing hospitality that we are provided for.

Just as it is in loving that we are loved

it is in giving that we receive;

It is in pardoning that we are pardoned;

and it is in dying to self that we are born again to eternal life.

Mary, Did You Know?
Luke 1:26-55

Today is Mary's Sunday. Mary as in the mother of Jesus, bride of Joseph, the 15-year-old girl who gave birth to the savior of the world. It is in her honor that the fourth advent candle is pink--that's as close as we protestants get to venerating the woman who in other traditions is called the Holy Mother, or Theotokos--God bearer.

Though perhaps it is high time that we recognized what a significant influence Mary has had on all of us--this young, poor, marginal, pregnant out of wedlock woman. Today is a day to remember Mary's legacy.

But first, a quick poll this morning. Raise your hand if you are a woman and you love musicals. I know it seems like a non-sequitur but go with it. Musicals--as in plays or movies where people inexplicably break out in song. Women, you love these, don't you? Come on, admit it. Now for the men. Okay--plenty of men here love musicals too. Still, I'm going to say that as a general patriarchal stereotype man get less excited about musicals than women. Myself included, though clearly you all are influencing me--I was watching a TV show the other week where the characters started singing for no good reason, and I found it charming. "Oh, isn't that cute--Oh they're so funny and talented, and OH what costumes!" But most men, not so much.

So, I find it a bit odd--you might even say joyfully queer, that this is an aspect of Luke's gospel. How Mary just bursts out in song--she just can't help herself. And then later Zechariah has his solo, and then in another scene the angels have their go. It's all very dramatic, very festive, so very unlike what you would expect from a serious story about the birth of the savior of the world. John the righteous Baptist--now there's a manly main character. Herod killing babies--a very violent, stereotypically masculine plot. But what are these two silly singing women doing in the script? Didn't the men who wrote this stuff down know that patriarchy isn't big on musical theater? And how did the ancient scribes and the theologians --mostly men-- how did they manage to put up with this stuff and continue to pass it along?

And yet here it is. The whole birth narrative is so dramatic, it's almost impossible to imagine it without a musical score--no wonder pageantry is all the rage this time of year. The Angel Gabriel from heaven came, his wings as drifted snow, and his eyes aflame." And sweet little Mary looks over her shoulder and says, "What, you're here for me? How can this be. . .?"

But clearly Mary is the star of the show. Innocent, naïve little Mary responds to the angel with quiet courage:

"Let it be with me according to your word." Even though having a child out of wedlock would have branded her a harlot, a loose woman, a shame to her family. Even though she was given no assurances that her fiancé would stand by her. What if David cut and run? Who would believe her story of being visited by an Angel? What if Mary was to bear this child alone, destitute--this announcement could have felt to her like a death sentence.

But we're not given any of these psychological details in scripture. We have to rely on modern drama for that kind of telling. Perhaps because the men who wrote down this story weren't all that concerned about how Mary felt about what was happening to her. In Mary's time women were considered necessary for child-bearing, obviously, but they were also thought to be overly emotional, too dramatic for much else. For goodness sake, they'd say, let's not dwell on how they feel. Better to talk about the genealogy of the groom, perhaps the geopolitics of the situation--the forced census, the poverty of the shepherds, the lack of affordable housing in Bethlehem. We men like to count things--I mean people--and talk about how much things cost, but let's not dwell on all the touchy-feely women's business. You see what I'm saying?

So, no wonder Mary probably felt the need to get out of town for a minute. I imagine she got tired of being treated like an object in her hometown. With all the people pointing and staring at her growing mid-section. Even strangers coming up and touching her belly as if it didn't belong to her, saying stupid things about how she is positively "glowing" and how it must be a girl because of the way she was carrying the weight, and "When was she due?" As if she would tell them what the Angel had said. These people were driving her crazy!

So, Mary did what any reasonable woman would do in that situation. She sought out the company of another woman, in this case Elizabeth, her relative who lived out in the country. Praise God that the Angel had at least tipped her off that Elizabeth might understand. As soon as Mary opened the door, it was like "oh, Honey, come here." And Mary would have wept for joy were it not for the boys getting all excited in-utero. John with his kicking and pointing. Jesus clearly trying to give his cousin a high-five. At least we men can get excited about the belly kicks, right? I'm thinking that's why this little anecdote got left in the story--even we know that this is cause for celebration.

First Elizabeth breaks out in song. She's like "Mary, did you know that your Baby Boy would one day walk on water?"

And then the back-up singers start: "Mary, did you know that your Baby Boy would save our sons and daughters?"

But then Mary steps in and she's like, "Oh no, you don't, this is MY time to shine," And when Mary starts to sing. Oh, Lord, it's like nothing we've ever heard. In that moment, now that the men are all gone, and the light is just on her, little Mary finds her voice. And what a voice!

It's like she's channeling the greatest prophets of her people. But not the prophets we often remember--not Isaiah or Jeremiah or Moses or Daniel. The Holy Spirit gives Mary the voice of her female ancestors of faith--the mothers of her people. The cries of Hannah and Esther and Miriam. The words of Deborah and Vashti and Rebeccah and Ruth. This was a song, a melody, that had been carried through the generations of her people, now finding a voice in a little girl from Nazareth, who was bringing to birth the salvation of the world.

"My heart cries out", she sang. "My heart cries out with a joyful shout that the God of my heart is great! The Lord has called me, a little girl from Nazareth, and now forever people will call me blessed--even though I'm poor and a teenage mother and unknown. And you know what this means? God has brought down the powerful from their thrones and lifted the lowly; God has filled the hungry with good thing and sent the rich away empty. God has helped all our people, according to the promise made to our ancestors, long ago."

Many people have tried to put these words to song, but I don't think any of today's melodies ever seem to do it justice, this Magnificat--this amazing prophetic song of Mary. What does do it justice is when we see and acknowledge the ways that this prophecy is true. When we celebrate that Mary was and is right --how God HAS done great things for us, not just for her, but for all of us. How God's mercies are abundant from Generation to Generation, even when the night is long and dark, and it seems like we are far from blessed.

Though she herself was living through a difficult and dangerous time, little mother Mary sings of the greatness of our God. And note how she sings of what God has already done for her. All these verbs are past tense. It's not what God *will* do, how God *will* turn the world upside down, lift the humble, bring down the proud. Mary sings as though it has already happened-- Jesus is still in the womb, but she sings as though salvation is *already* a done deal, because it *was*! Because it *is*. And the presence of this brilliantly subversive feminine story is itself a sign for us, that the Lord of Glory is continuing to do what Mary sang about--to redeem God's people and set us free.

Here's what I mean by that: When Jesus died on the cross and rose three days later, we know that the powers of sin and death were defeated, but it's not like all oppression and injustice suddenly ceased to exist. That would have been great if suddenly, all the wars were ended, and all people were instantly reconciled to one another, to God, and to the earth, but that didn't happen. Instead there seems to be a longer plan in the works. It seems more like Jesus was the tipping point in God's mission to save our world. Jesus won the decisive battle, he put a crack in the foundation of evil that would someday bring down the whole house, the whole structure of injustice. We know that in Jesus, the climax of the story has come already, but the show isn't over just yet.

Often the hardest thing in our lives is maintaining hope during this already, but not-yet kind of time that Mary was in. It can feel at times as though, like Mary, we are marginalized, isolated, abandoned--we can feel so alone. We can feel crushed by feelings of loss or failure, hopelessness. We can feel oppressed by structures of racism, patriarchy, or corporate greed. But along comes Mary, with her wildly subversive and hopeful song. I like to imagine her laughing and dancing along with Elizabeth in that hill country. "The Hills are alive, with the sound of music." Singing and rejoicing because God has already won the victory--and the powers of her day don't even know it yet. They don't realize that it may be Friday, but Sunday's coming! Justice is coming. Vindication is coming. Salvation is coming, and it is already here, because the God of Creation has visited God's people and set us free.

It was a couple thousand years ago that Mary and Elizabeth got together for this little musical. It was essentially around that time that the term Patriarchy was coined, since it originally referred to the family system in the Roman empire in which fathers had absolute rule. I like to think that Mary was laughing and singing that day because she could see the end of that system--the roots of its demise in the child of her womb. Here was coming a teacher who would welcome women to be his students, a religious leader who would affirm the gifts of his female followers--Jesus would be a savior who would champion the rights of women and re-establish women's status as equal children of God. It's not like Patriarchy went away the day Jesus went up into heaven, but over the centuries, followers of Jesus have continued to rediscover his egalitarian intent and spread the good news that we all get to dance and sing in the Kingdom of God. Because there is no room for

Patriarchy in the Beloved Community. There is no room for marginalization or domination or oppression of any kind.

And the amazing thing about singing this song in 2014, is that we have so many signs that this age is close to coming in full. When women are and will continue to be lifted, along with all their many gifts and sometimes musical preferences. There was a popular article in the Atlantic a few years ago that was turned into a book--it's called the "End of Men. "If you haven't read it, it's still available via google. The author, Hanna Rosin, has started talking about the 21st century as the century of women, because it seems the modern, post-industrial economy is better suited toward women than toward men. For instance, in 2010, women became the majority of the workforce for the first time in US History. Most managers are now women too. And for every two men who get a college degree these days, three women will do the same. We know we have a long way to go before women get equal pay for equal work and break through the corporate and political glass ceiling. But we know it's coming, don't we? That ceiling was cracked 2000 years ago, Friends, by Mary and her Magnificent song, so and it's only a matter of time. Just a matter of time before we are all laughing and singing again like she was.

Like her, we get to sing and dance and make Merry this Christmas no matter how things are going in this temporal time, because we know that God is on the move and soon will be here. There will be no more crying in that age to come. No more dying there. When Jesus is among us. There will be no war, no pain, no loneliness, no fear. Only the songs of the saints and the rejoicing of the angels. When Mary's child is born. Amen?

Emmanuel
Luke 2:1-20

I say Emmanuel, you say God is with us. Immanuel! **God is with us.** Immanuel! **God is with us.** Indeed, God is with us. It's been a rough year, 2017. A troubling year. But we come together tonight to remember that God is still with us.

Just like God was with the people in that dark reign of empire so many centuries ago when these gospels were written. When Emperors made people register with the government, to prove where they were from. They did it so that they could get more taxes from poor people in order to give more money to rich people. And, so the emperor could deport the people he didn't want within his borders. It sounds familiar, doesn't it? The ways of empire? This is the context in which we are reminded of Emmanuel. **God is with us!**

We can imagine what it would be like for this poor young couple--Jo the contractor and Mary, his pregnant teenage fiancé. We can picture them struggling to get things together for a shotgun wedding when they are suddenly forced to make an uncomfortable trip to their hometown to get some documents in order. And when they get there it turns out there are no rooms available--at least none that they can afford. Bethlehem is so popular suddenly. Today we might call this gentrification--they just thought of it as a lack of hospitality—the way native people were forced to take shelter in a barn; a pregnant woman left out in the cold, homeless. This is the society we find ourselves in when the messenger says Emmanuel. **God is with us!**

It must have been uncomfortable for poor little pregnant Mary, riding for days on a donkey when she was about to pop. But what did that gold-plated Emperor care about women's bodies? Our Molester-in-chief also wouldn't care that Mary's baby would be born surrounded by farm animals, without the assistance of midwife or doctor. He doesn't think these kinds of people should have healthcare at all. And yet still Jesus is born. They called him Emmanuel. **God is with us!**

The announcement came in the middle of the night, not on Wall Street, not at the White House or the penthouse or even city hall, but it was a bunch of working-class people who heard it first. People who had to take jobs at night because they couldn't find any during the day. They were probably guys with records, making minimum wage to provide security for a bunch of sheep, even though this contract work didn't make them feel very secure. Still, the messenger came to THEM, said "don't be afraid, I've got good news." Emmanuel. **God is with us!**

Who us? Said the shepherds. Who us? Said Mary and Jo. Mary pondered these things in her heart. Others that night were thinking about the status of Jerusalem, and about how the government would be funded after the census numbers came in. It might have been sensible for this family to think about their own legal status—maybe heading to Egypt to escape this deranged Emperor and his destructive decrees. But on that night at least, all Mary could think about was this baby, and what people were saying about him. They called him Emmanuel. **God is with us.**

And this child could change everything. Everything! Maybe not instantly. Maybe not all at once. But as that awareness grows--as the news continues to spread that God is with the people. With the poor ones. With the forgotten ones. With the least and the lost and the lonely ones. That the God of all creation is also with US! Mary pictured that baby getting bigger and bigger, bringing life and light to everyone he met. Maybe someday even doing something about those Roman publicans who treated them like dirt. Mary looked at Jesus' beautiful, innocent little face. And she smiled.

This is the word of the Lord. **Thanks be to God.**

The Disturbing Word
John 1

"In the beginning was the word and the word was with God, and the word was God." These opening lines from the gospel of John have become so famous and common-place in the church that we sometimes forget how radical they were when they were first written down. Originally, they were meant to be revolutionary. Maybe a bit like the Declaration of Independence in our country. We tend to know part of that opening also: "We hold these truths to be self-evident, that all men are created equal, endowed by their Creator with certain inalienable rights." These words likewise were intended to declare independence from a foreign empire. They were meant to be fighting words! It helps to hear the words before them. The American declaration actually begins with "When in the course of human events it becomes necessary for one people to dissolve the political bands which have connected them to another. . .". Then they declare the "causes that impel them to separate"—as in our inalienable rights. Context is everything.

Likewise, in this declaration of St John, there is a context for the poetic prologue to the Word, laid out in all the biblical writings that came before. For those of us who have been following along with this writing since September, we know it to be a history of bloodshed and idolatry and oppression. From the patriarchs through the prophets, from dysfunctional families to domineering empires, God's people are seen to have suffered and struggled and done their level best to get back to the relationship with God that they'd hoped and dreamed of—that idyllic paradise written about in the book of Genesis—in the beginning. But it had never worked. Nothing had worked. They'd tried monarchy, but the kings had been oppressive. They'd tried the temple, but the priests had been no better. They'd tried personal piety and wisdom and private devotion to God, but still it wasn't enough. Still it felt like God was absent--nowhere to be seen.

So, when Jesus and his disciples came along, preaching about this different so-called "way" of the kingdom of God, the people of the time were understandable skeptical. Because what they were talking about sounded new and novel and untested. "Who is this Jesus character anyway?" They said. "We've never read about him before. We've heard about Abraham and Moses and David and Isaiah—we know about those men who spoke and taught the word of God, but nothing is written about a man from Nazareth. What authority does this Jesus guy have to speak against our monarchy, and our temple, and our system of ritual purity?" They rejected him because his teaching felt new and different.

Incidentally, have you ever rejected information because it was new or different from what you'd been taught? Because it came across as a bit too radical or revolutionary? It seems like this is kind of a common reaction. Some famous examples come to mind. Remember how people like Copernicus and Galileo tried to tell everybody that world is round, but then most people at the time said, "Ahh, no. That doesn't sound right. I've never heard that before." Same thing with Darwin—some people still struggle with the whole idea of evolution even though we have mountains of books written about it. Still they say, "No—that's not what my parents taught me—that's not how it was in the beginning." Likewise, today the main issue is global warming. It's caused by humans—we know this—there is a consensus in the scientific community, and yet still we have an administration in the whitehouse that is unwilling to accept this new information. Unfortunately, we all tend reject information that is inconvenient to us—news that doesn't fit with our beliefs and preferences around things like parenting, investing, Sabbath, prayer. Jesus said to some skeptics once, he said, "Destroy this temple and in three days I'll raise it up again." But they said to him, "Yeah right. It took decades to build that temple. Where is your evidence? Where are your peer reviewed articles?" And we probably would have said the same thing to Jesus, don't you think?

This new Word of Jesus--The Word--is different and therefore disturbing to the status quo, in a revolutionary kind of way. Kind of like the way a new baby in the family tends to mess with established routines. Once that infant comes home, everything is chaos for a while. The parents duke it out over conflicting habits from their families of origin, while siblings compete for attention with this new little distraction. Jesus can really shake things up just by virtue of being new!

So, St John in his declaration of revolution takes us back to the beginning, to the book of Genesis, using the same words to tell us about this new ancient WORD. "In the beginning" says some of the oldest and most venerated writing on earth. In the beginning says John, the Word that we have known in Christ Jesus was with God and the word was God. Sometimes it feels like the things he says to us through the Holy Spirit are brand new, but they're as old as creation, because he spoke them into being. Everything came into being through him. St Paul said that everything he'd thought to be true about the world—all the principles and absolutes he lived his life by previously—all of that he considered to be garbage after meeting the Risen Jesus. Because it turns out that Jesus was and is the way, the truth and the life. His was the word that humanity had been trying to discern all along—he's not new to the world, he's simply the one that makes all things feel new! He's the one that rocks our world and makes us reconsider everything we've ever known. And he does this to us over, and over, and over again.

Every time that baby Jesus comes back to the house it's like we're in diapers again. It's exhausting, isn't it? This Word made flesh among us? At Christmas Jesus is the baby, and yet somehow, we are the ones who end up feeling like children. Somehow, he makes it possible for us to begin again—to go back to the beginning, even to become a new creation!

St John's gospel implies that not everyone does this. It's too hard for some people to take in new information, to reinterpret everything they've ever known--to join in the revolution. But to those who receive this Word, who believe in his name rather than the names they've made for themselves. For those who believe what it says—often without statistics, without footnotes, just through innocent trust. For those who believe in this Word, Christ gives power to become children of God, just like him. Just like it was in the beginning, when God made Adam and Eve directly and they had no-one else to rely on but their creator. This Word of God is the key to getting back to that Garden. The way to salvation isn't the monarchy, it's not the temple, it's not even the wisdom tradition. Remember the context. St John is saying something new here. Before all these things were thought to be necessary, the Word of God was there. And now the word of God is here, among us, calling us back to a new beginning to become Children of God again.

And not just any children, but the kind that were intended from the beginning. St John lists three essential attributes of these children. Again, it's like that declaration of Independence—they said that America would guarantee a few things-- life, liberty and the pursuit of happiness. John also has three, but notice how different they are--how revolutionary:

First, the Word says that Children of God are not born of blood. Blood as in bloodshed, blood as in violence. Jesus' gospel is first and foremost a gospel of peace. There will be no harm done on all my holy mountain says the Lord of hosts. In this new beginning of the gospel, Cain doesn't kill his brother Abel again because the cycle of violence has been interrupted through Jesus' sacrifice. There will be no retribution, no vengeance, because this time forgiveness will reign. Can you imagine how different history would be if Christians through the centuries had been able to receive this essential non-violent word? Those who have ears, let them hear, the children of God are not born of blood. That's the first principle of this new kingdom—it's non-violent.

Secondly, the children of God aren't born of the will of the flesh either. The will of the flesh being the things that our bodies want that our consciences tell us we probably shouldn't have. Like our neighbor's Porsche or our neighbors' spouse or that second home we mortgaged while neglecting the homeless poor. The desire of the flesh is largely about materialism—the love of stuff, and the way we tend to treat other people like objects. It's not about denying the basic needs of the body, but when it comes to what we desire, Jesus is very clear that we can't serve both God and mammon, so being born of God means letting go of stuff. This is where it gets real on Christmas, right?

That's two out of three so far. The Word of God that we're celebrating this season is non-violent, it's anti-materialistic. It reminds me of Martin Luther King's famous giant triplets. Remember how he talked about opposing the three great evils of Militarism, Materialism, and . . . Racism?! Now there was a child of God! This wasn't a new word either—it was as old as creation, though spoken slightly differently.

St John has a slightly different take too. He says in this Christian manifesto that the Advent of God means that we can be born not of blood, or of the will of the flesh, or of the will of a man. "The will of a Man." Think about that. The word John uses here is intentionally masculine—just like we know now that the Declaration of Independence was written specifically by and for white men—not women or people of color. John's gospel is also conscious of social location but in the opposite direction. This prologue isn't talking about the will of a human being, it's calling out specifically the will of a man, because the Word of God stands against the evils of patriarchy! Jesus came to earth during the Roman Empire, where the rule of men, not women was considered divine. And so, the Word of our God stands against this. And always has. This isn't a new word. This isn't only true now that we've had the women's march on Washington and the #MeToo movement. From the beginning of creation God made men and women to be equal partners in caring for God's creation, but then evil happened. Men started exploiting and dominating women. And the system of patriarchy came to exploit men as well—LBGT children of God, people of other races and cultures—it all got rolled into an overarching system of domination in which men exerted their will on others. So the Word of God came back to earth, to breathe into a new creation that is not ruled by the will of any man, but only by the will of God, so that from now on there would be no Jew or Greek, no slave or free, no male or female, but that we would all be Children of God in Christ Jesus.

Wouldn't that be something? Wouldn't it be revolutionary?!! Just three main expectations of the children of God—non-violent, non-materialistic, nonpatriarchal. And all we must do to get there is believe that the Word of God can do what it says it can do. That as we trust in Jesus and live into this vision that has been with us from the beginning of the world, God saves us, God lifts us up, God even restores us to the abundant provision of that paradise in the garden of Eden. Is that what you see happening in Christmas? Do you see God putting flesh on these ideas for us—helping us to see and hear the Word anew through an innocent child, laid humbly in a manger?

Friends, I invite you to a new beginning this year. I invite you as St John does, to consider how the word has been with you from the very beginning, calling us all to new life as a child of God. I invite you to think and pray about how this word is taking on flesh around us today—what this re-newed, child-like faith may require of us, how we may have to reconsider everything that has gone before in the light of this Emmanuel--God's justice with us. In Christ Jesus we have seen the grace and truth and glory of God. So how now will we live as God's children? Without violence, without greed, without patriarchy. The revolution is here, friends. Believe the good news that the Word has come to make all things new. including us.

John the Baptist
Luke 3:1-22

In the 16th year of the war on terror, when Donald Trump was being sworn in as President of the United States and Exon CEO Rex Tillerson was preparing to be Secretary of State and Scott Pruitt was getting ready to dismantle the EPA, during the papacy of Francis of Argentina, when J Herbert Nelson II was stated clerk of the PCUSA,

The word of God came to a homeless guy named John who was camping out next to the little Naches river outside of Yakama.

Over the course of many months John went into the cities and towns on all sides of Mt Rainier, standing on street corners, wandering through strip malls, announcing to anyone who would listen, a so-called "baptism of repentance for the forgiveness of sins."

He would preach from memory out of the book of Isaiah, claiming to be, quote "The voice of one crying out in the wilderness."

His message was simple: "God is coming!" he would say. "Get ready to meet your maker! Straighten things out while you still have a chance!"

At first people ignored this strange fellow—from the way he dressed it was clear that he had been living off the land, and from the way he spoke and carried himself you could tell he had gone a long time without interacting with others. The man was clearly a bit "different" as we like to say, maybe even a bit "special." But after he kept popping up consistently in town after town without injury or illness, John began to get noticed, and he even achieved a bit of notoriety via social media. Not quite the stature of your John 3:16 guy at football games, but still, this John eventually merited his own hashtag. At first, they called him "Isaiah guy" on account of his choice of scripture. But then someone finally asked him his name and they updated it to #John-the-baptizer. After that it suddenly became a thing to post a selfie with crazy guy. And then when a few teenagers thought it would be cool to take John up on his offer of baptism, John even managed to develop somewhat of a cult following out in the desert near where he'd been staying—it grew to rival the likes of Burning Man NW.

All this attention, you'd think, would have pleased John-the-baptizer, but it didn't. Once things really started getting out of hand and John started to see certain politicians and corporate execs trying to capitalize on the action, he lost his cool a little bit. Sometimes John would randomly start yelling at the crowd, "You brood of snakes! Who warned you to flee from the wrath to come!" And he'd shake a bony finger at them, which of course only made the people that much more enamored with him. And amazingly they listened to what he had to say.

"Bear fruits worthy of repentance!" John would say to them. And the folk who grew up on the farms outside of Yakima understood him completely. They knew all about good fruit and bad fruit. If your trees aren't producing good fruit, you use your tractors to tear them out of the ground, and then you pile them up and burn them. And then when you plant new trees, you sure as better make sure they're the right variety, because it takes years for them to bear fruit again. So, they got it--if you're going to make a change, make sure it's for the right reasons and that you're going to get good results. Those farmers loved the way this John the Baptizer was talking.

And the young people loved him too. "This dude is righteous" they said to each other. "Finally, someone who tells it like it is and lives it!" So, word continued to spread that John was the real deal. One guy got some signs, saying "John the Baptizer for President." And people started to ask him, seriously, what it is he thought they should do differently.

And John had a consistently simple answer for them. "Well," he'd say, "If you have two coats, then give one to somebody who doesn't have one. Do the same with your food. Share what you have. Period" This, of course wasn't hard teaching to grasp, but some people tried to complicate it. Like the news reporter who flew in from Seattle to cover the story.

"So, ah, John Baptist, is it? People are saying you're in favor of redistribution, that you might even be preaching communism to the people out here. Is that right?" But John wasn't interested in all of that. "What I said was, if you have two coats, and someone else doesn't have one, then give the person your coat. It's the same with food."

"Well what about money? Are you suggesting we give away our money too?"

"I said coats and food."

"But what happens when everyone is clothed and fed?"

"When do you think that will happen?"

"I see, well thank you for your time, sir."

Apparently, this simple teaching was rather challenging for some. But nevertheless, it seemed to appeal to a wide variety of people. Rich people, poor people, young and old, people of various religions and backgrounds and identities.

Even some corporate bankers showed up in the desert looking to make a change. As they would come to the front of the baptismal line and wade down into the still frosty waters of the little Naches river, they would ask him,

"Teacher, what should WE do differently?" Everyone in the crowd expected John to turn them away, or tell them to quit their jobs, but instead he simply told them not to cheat anyone. "Don't try to trick anybody into a mortgage they can't afford," he said, "and don't try to collect any more interest than is fair." The people were amazed.

Some Lawyers were in line for baptism also. "What should we do?" They said. And John said to them,

"Don't extort money from anyone---don't make threats or false accusations and be satisfied with your wages."

All this back and forth only built up John's reputation further, and no one was making fun of his horse hair sweater anymore. The whole crowd was wondering if John was the guru, they'd all been waiting for. "Finally, a religious leader we can trust!" They said to each other.

But John wasn't interested in starting another mega-church or even a franchise. "Look," he said to the crowd. "I baptize with water so that you can get cleaned up and turn your lives around, but the important thing is that God is on the way. The one who's coming after me is going to go way further. He baptizes with the Holy Spirit and with fire! He has the power to sort the good from the bad in your life and purify you completely and LIGHT YOU UP."

The crowd wasn't entirely sure what this meant, of course, but they shouted and cheered because clearly John meant it as good news. If John was good and righteous, then this messiah person must be that much better!

So, imagine the enthusiasm when the next day John saw his cousin Jesus coming down to the water and pointed to him. John announced to the crowd, "Behold, the Lamb of God, who takes away the sins of the whole world!" It was pandemonium. This guy Jesus, though, he was super unassuming. John thought Jesus was going to take over the baptizing and what not right away, but instead he insisted on being baptized himself, along with the rest of the people, so that he would know what that cold water felt like, soaking him down to the bone.

But, just as John had said, there did end up being something different about Jesus' baptism. There was a lot going on that day, so the reports are mixed as to when it happened, or exactly what it looked like or sounded like, but everyone agrees that God showed up in a special way at Jesus' baptism. First Jesus waded out into that chilly river to stand next to the baptizer. The water was flowing pretty good, ready to wash away any sins that might have clung to him, though they say Jesus didn't have any flaws that needed washing anyway. As he was standing there, I wonder if Jesus thought about the waters of creation—if the crowds and the chaos reminded him of that first day when God made the heavens and the earth, the building-blocks of a new creation. And as the baptizer pushed him down under the water, I wonder if the person said, like we sometimes say, "the old is dead and gone," and when he came up from the water, I wonder if Jesus thought about Noah and his family, coming out of the waters of the flood into a new covenant, a new life with God, or if he pictured Moses and the people of Israel coming up out of the recently parted red sea, victorious over death, free at last. I wonder if the baptizer said to Jesus, "Behold, a new life has begun!"

Unfortunately, we don't know all the details of his baptism, because everything was overshadowed at that point by the appearance of the Holy Spirit. After Jesus had come out of the water and was praying, something like a dove came down and landed on him, and voice came from heaven, saying "You are my son, the Beloved, with you I am well pleased!"

And that was that. The rest of the gathering was completely anti-climactic. I heard a few people took off with Jesus, after they saw that he was the one John was preparing people for—the one with an even better baptism. It was just a few poor kids who chose to follow him, though, so most people didn't even notice when they left. And then crowd died down. I imagine most of them just sort of went home after they got dipped. Maybe they got some tee-shirts made, "Baptizmalpalooza, 2017," but for some reason for the most part, the repentance part didn't stick. A few months later and it was like just another failed New-Year's resolution, memorialized in cheap cotton and eventually sent to the Goodwill in order to make room for the next year's fad. When the people remembered their baptisms, they'd think to themselves, "Sure, giving away food and clothing is a good idea, but who has the time for all of that when you live in the real world? If John wants to be a minimalist or a philanthropist or whatever, more power to him, but not everyone can live like that. I've got a family to take care of, you know?" So, one by one they all made their excuses. And again, John was left alone, with nothing but a Facebook page and a few followers on twitter.

The next year it made the news that John was in prison—apparently convicted on some trumped-up charge related to criticizing who the President was in bed with. And John got pretty discouraged out there behind bars at Monroe, as people often do. Because even more of the people he had baptized turned away from him. "John," they would say, "We were with you when it was all about charity, but why'd you have to go and get all political on us?"

And John cried out to God, because he realized that the crowd had never really understood. They hadn't gotten it—that the personal IS political. He wrote to Jesus, to find out how things were going on the outside. And in the letter John couldn't help but admit that he was having his doubts about the mission. Had he squandered his life seeking the Beloved Community? Was all that baptizing out in the desert for nothing? "Are you even the one we've been waiting for," he wrote to Jesus, "or should we be looking for someone else?"

Jesus was on a tour of his own by that point, so he couldn't write back himself, but he sent a report to the prison through some friends. John opened the envelope, unfolded the simple letter and began to read. It said, "Dear Teacher John, this is what we've seen and heard: The blind are receiving sight, people who couldn't walk before are running and jumping, those who had nasty diseases are being cleansed, the deaf can hear, the dead are raised, and the good news is proclaimed to the poor."

John put down that letter and he wept. He wept for joy. He wept with hope. Because the work wasn't in vain. The movement wasn't over. It was just getting started. The Kingdom of God was at hand. The people of God had received salvation, and the best was yet to come.

Rising to Serve
Mark 1:29-39

This morning I want to begin by telling you about the woman on the cover of your bulletin--one of the sometimes-forgotten ancestors of faith. Alberta Christine Williams was born in 1904 to the pastor of Ebenezer Baptist Church in Atlanta Georgia. She studied to become a teacher and taught for a short while before getting married in 1926 to a man who would also become the pastor of Ebenezer Baptist Church. Together they had three children-- two boys and a girl, and in addition to taking care of the kids while her husband cared for the church, Alberta was president of the Ebenezer Women's Committee, and as a talented musician she served as choir director and church organist. Sadly, Alberta only lived to about 70 years old. She was shot and killed on June 30th, 1974 while she was playing the organ in church. The 23-year-old man who did it said he had decided that all Christians were his enemies, and he had targeted the pastor because he thought black ministers were a menace to black people. Then he had changed his mind and shot Alberta instead because he thought it would cause her husband more pain. This man who martyred Alberta was sentenced to death, but it was later commuted to life in prison due to advocacy on the part of family since Alberta had herself been opposed to the death penalty. Also sad was the fact that Alberta had been preceded in death by her youngest child Alfred, also a pastor--she was a pastor's mother! And before that she had lost her middle child, Martin, who was also a pastor of some renown. Didn't Alberta Williams King have a remarkable life? Doesn't it sound like she must have been an amazing woman? Who would Rev. Dr. King have been without his mother? She herself had quite a story, and yet we forget her, because she served quietly in the background while others claimed the spotlight.

Today's gospel passage includes another such story, about a woman whose service perhaps also deserves a little more attention than we've given her in the past.

As usual there aren't a whole lot of details in the account given to us in the Gospel of Mark. Jesus, you may remember from last week, had just gotten done casting out an unclean spirit at worship in the synagogue. After that he went to the home of a couple of his disciples--Simon and his brother Andrew. Maybe he went there because all that exorcism business had wiped him out and he needed a little R&R--I'm thinking just a power nap, because you know, this is Jesus. Or maybe he was hungry because it had been a long time since breakfast and Simon's place had the best Saturday brunch-who knows.

Anyway, Jesus gets to the house and it turns out that there is an unclean spirit there too. It's like they're everywhere, these unclean spirits. Can't a savior get some peace? Only this one manifests as a fever. At that time, they thought that fevers were caused by unclean spirits, you see--so it was all the same to them--the one at the Synagogue, the one at Simon's house.

But it turned out that this one was disturbing Simon's mother-in-law. And this was a big problem, obviously--I mean if she's sick, well then there's nobody to cook the brunch, and then nobody gets a good nap, right?

But fortunately, Jesus doesn't even sweat it. Immediately he goes into the room where the older woman is laying, takes her by the hand and lifts her up. I imagine she had to be a bit wobbly on her feet, but then, sure enough, the fever is gone, and all the people in the house are like "Hooray! It's a miracle! She's saved!" Only here's the kicker. As soon as the fever is gone, she starts to serve them--Jesus and his merry band of disciples. She rises to serve. And the men go on about their business.

And as we read this story today with our critical lenses on, this can seem a bit strange, if not a bit sexist--especially the way I've described it so far. So, Jesus gets this sick old woman out of bed, so she'll make them something to eat? "Get up and serve me, woman!" Right? We aren't told her name, we aren't told anything about her besides her relationship to the head of the household--in this case her son Simon, and then her only part to play in the story is to serve the men. Huh. I wonder what happened to Simon's mother-in-law later. Did she become a follower of Jesus? Did the crowds later turn on her the way they turned on Jesus and his disciples? We don't get to hear about any of that. You've got to wonder, particularly once Simon became known as the Apostle Peter, did she suffer as he suffered, or at least as Mary the mother of Jesus Suffered? There are probably traditions around this--stories here and there. But we'll probably never know for certain--her story is mostly lost, as are the stories of so many of our ancestors of faith.

And yet I wonder if this isn't also part of the point being made in this simple story--one that the author of this story was quite conscious of--St Mark is intentional about pretty much every word he uses--perhaps his point is that the gospel isn't so much about us and our stories as it is about Jesus and his kingdom. And considering that fact I wonder if service isn't what this woman might have wanted to be remembered for too.

Consider this with your sanctified imaginations--here's another way it could have gone down. It may have been that Simon-Peter's mother-in-law wasn't even really that sick--the whole thing happens so fast. I picture an old woman splayed out on the couch, moaning and groaning. "Children, Children, my head my head, here I am close to death, but do they care? Simon and his brother are out on the town with their friends. All I do is wait on these children hand and foot, but do they ever care for me, eh, an old dying woman?"

But then Jesus comes in and sees her and takes her hand, and he lifts her up--body and soul, and suddenly, she's back on task. The men are saying "Take it easy Mrs. -err Simon's mother-in-law, you just relax." But she's not having any of it. "Fever, what fever, oh it's nothing, nothing could keep me from serving, Jesus! That's what I'm here to do."

Incidentally, does that remind you of anyone you've perhaps known? We all know people like this, don't we? People with servants' hearts who want nothing more than to help somebody. What do YOU think this woman was like? Can you picture her like Rosa Parks--taking a break on a bus and then that's all she gets remembered for? Or was she just always in the kitchen like your great aunt Bertha? Was she more like Flossie or Marla or Alberta Christine King? We don't really know. All we know is that miracle or no miracle, this woman rises to serve Jesus, so that he can then serve the crowds who come to the house that night--themselves in search of healing. And that is something amazing, isn't it? How her service becomes part of Jesus' story--The Gospel.

The next day in this story, early in the morning, Jesus gets away for a bit, maybe out praying, maybe just needing to get out of that crowded house, and when his disciples find him, he is ready to go again, saying "Let's take our message out to the neighboring towns too since that's what I'm here to do." He rises to serve. It's like he's taking his cue from the old woman. In this story Peter's mother-in-law is portrayed as the model for what Jesus himself does--giving himself over to service without much concern for his own welfare. He too rises to serve, because that's who he is. No one forces this woman to serve, any more than Jesus needs someone to tell him to get going. It turns out that this woman is the model disciple, the first deacon, a person for whom Jesus would no doubt have great praise, if the Gospel of Mark was long enough to include those kinds of details.

As it is, we must read through the lines a bit, in order to avoid letting this narrative come across as too patriarchal. Again, we don't know much about Simon Peter's mother-in-law, but we know enough to be able to compare her to the men in her household. Here's a woman whose first thought after recovering from illness is to serve others, while Peter, Andrew, James, and John, what do we hear them doing in the story? Arguing about who is the greatest! "Who is the greatest among us, Jesus?" They say, "Let me be on your right hand when you come into power, Jesus." And what does Jesus say to them? The greatest among you is the one who serves. If you want to be great in God's kingdom, become the servant of all." It's no wonder this woman doesn't get more mention in the gospels--that would have been particularly embarrassing, given the way the men are behaving. "Why can't you be more like your mother-in-law, huh, Peter?" Wouldn't it be funny if we got to the pearly gates, and it was this woman with the list of names rather than St Peter? I generally don't find that kind of imagery helpful, but there could be a lot of surprises in store for us, that's all I'm saying.

And it seems to me that we would be wise to think a little more on this model of quiet service, given that Jesus endorses this pattern over and against the normal ways of the world, in which service is considered servile, and we for the most part act as if life is about being served rather than pouring out our lives in service to others.

A few things I'll point out that I think we can glean from this story before I close:

First, this is a story about the home because that's where service begins--in the home, with those closest to us. Women often understand this better than men. I've been learning this with my children recently, what a joy it is to serve them, but also what a responsibility it is to teach them to serve also, because their lives will be diminished if they don't also learn how to serve. I read in this parenting book about how you should have your kids clear the table after meals as a way for them to express gratitude and to make them feel like an important part of the household. At first, I had a hard time with this. For one thing, supervising children as they try to juggle glassware can be a bit stressful, but it also just feels strange--expecting people half your size to wait on you. But since trying this out my older son has since moved on to washing a few dishes and even making some of his own meals to the point where one day when I realize that this gave me an extra 10 minutes in my day, I said to myself, "Hey, this isn't so bad!" And more than that, now he's more grateful for the times when I do serve him--now that he's learned to serve a little bit too. This can be true for all of us. These are habits we can learn and develop in our own homes.

The second thing about this story worth keeping in mind is that idea that servants also need to learn how to be served occasionally. This woman needed Jesus' healing touch in order to resume her service, didn't she? It may have been that she began serving because Jesus had lifted her up. Her service was fueled by gratitude for what God had done for her. And this type of gratitude can fuel our service also--remembering what God has done for us. Everybody needs a little help sometimes. Everybody needs a little encouragement, a helping hand, someone to lift you up and help you to stand. So, if that's you, then get used to it. Learn how to accept that hand of grace. Because if you're doing all the work, not only is it unfair to you and likely to burn you out, it is unfair to the other people who could be benefiting from the joy of serving others. Never forget that service is a gift, an opportunity-- it is our job as Christians to highlight and underscore this point, so that we'll all be scrambling to serve each other rather than walking over people as we try to serve ourselves. This is the heart of the kingdom of God, taught to us by people like Peter's mother-in-law. Serve and be served.

I read a poem posted on a door once--it turns out it is by Khalil Gibran:

"I slept, and I dreamed that life is all joy.

I woke, and I saw that life is all service.

I served, and I saw that service is joy."

Let me say that again--service is joy. So, don't hide it, and don't hoard it. If you've been doing the same volunteer gig for years and years, you might need to take a break. Invite someone else into the joy of that service. Then find another way to serve and be served.

That brings me to point three from this simple yet beautiful story of service. Service is a path that leads toward life. If you want a better life, a more fulfilling life, maybe even a long life, then always be on the lookout for ways to serve. If you need evidence of this truth, look no further than the elderly members of this congregation. Longevity seems to be a tradition in this place, in part because people here have dedicated their lives to serving others. Here are people who know that serving others can help lift you out of grief, out of depression. There are people here who I won't name because they are modest, perhaps like Simon Peter's mother-in-law, who keep going, who find strength during trial, who persevere over the long haul because they have a purpose beyond themselves in serving others. These are people who say, "I have to get up, because so and so needs me." "I have to get back to work, back to church, because my service matters." Often it doesn't even matter what that service is. You can bake pies, you can clean toilets, you can write cards or lead political campaigns. Martin Luther King Jr used to say it well-- I wonder if his mother taught him this, he said that

"Everybody can be great...because anybody can serve. You don't have to have a college degree to serve. You don't have to make your subject and verb agree to serve. You only need a heart full of grace. A soul generated by love."

And by this standard--when service is our goal rather than glory or honor, then we are more likely to succeed. At the end of days Jesus isn't going to say to anybody, "come into my kingdom, my great and accomplished hero, my rich and powerful one." No. Jesus will say to those on his right hand, "Come share in the joy of my master, my good and faithful servant, God's beloved child."

One final point from this passage, since it's such an important one, I'm going to say it again. The beautiful thing about the kingdom is that it's often the least of these who teach us about what is most important. In this story it's a nameless, marginalized woman who exemplifies discipleship. In our stories it is often the nameless, forgotten people who do the most important work among us. The gospel, friends, isn't just about remembering these people or honoring them. This is important too--we can honor those who have come before us and those who quietly serve among us today. But let's express our gratitude for them by following their example in service--by living our lives also with the kind of faithfulness and dedication as they have displayed. As this woman in scripture expressed her gratitude by serving Jesus, let us express our gratitude for God's grace by serving God and other people, especially the least and the lost and the forgotten. Amen?

Wanted
Luke 15:1-32

Welcome back to our journey with Jesus this season through the gospel of Luke! We're so glad you made it to the party today! I know it's Lent, but don't forget that even during seasons of penitence and fasting, Sundays are still feast days. We're here to celebrate together the word of God, the feast of God, the good gifts of fellowship and community and hope. The Kingdom of God is a party. It's a party that we get welcomed back to again and again and again.

That's one theme from this famous chapter of Luke's gospel—life with God is a celebration. When the woman finds her lost coin, she throws a party. When the prodigal father finds his lost son, he throws a party. Man, I wish every time we went to worship it felt like a party. I wish every Sunday morning we had this sense that we were returning home to a place of welcome and celebration.

But I get that it's a little more complicated than that. Because even the best of parties can be hard sometimes. Have you ever gone to a party that didn't feel like much fun? What was it that fell short—the food, the music? Most of time when I'm not having a good time at a party it's usually because of the people. It's almost always about the people. If it didn't go well, I often think, "They just weren't my kind of people." Have you ever felt that way? I know it's a bit shameful to admit, but when you don't connect with the people, you feel out of place. You don't feel welcome in the same way—it doesn't feel comfortable, it's not like a home-coming at all. I know that's something we struggle with here in our congregation too. I can see it in the faces of the visitors who come to check us out each week. Congregational consultants say that most people who are church shopping know within the first 2 minutes whether it's a good fit. And my guess is that this has a lot to do with who else is in the pews. And unfortunately, I see this same discomfort sometimes in the faces of those who have been worshiping here for many years, when they look around and notice that so many of the faces are new. Suddenly it doesn't feel as familiar, as comfortable—sometimes we don't feel welcome in our own church because the people have changed. It makes it harder to enjoy the party when we ourselves feel like strangers.

And yet that's the way this party is sometimes. It's hard, but it's true. That's how the Kingdom of God goes. The Beloved Community isn't necessarily made up just of the people who we already know or even the people we particularly like. The guest list isn't meant to be up to us at all—because it's

God's party, not ours. Which is frustrating to many people, even though Jesus made this clear from the very beginning.

That's what Jesus is doing in this chapter of Luke. Here we see some religious types complaining about the people Jesus was hanging out with. The same thing happened before with the woman who washed Jesus' feet with her hair, if you remember that story. The other guests didn't like her. And this theme keeps coming up. People keep complaining about all the "sinners" that Jesus invites to be a part of his community. Jesus seems to be most in his element when he's surrounded by foreigners and former criminals and people with mental health problems. Jesus is particularly attracted to the poor and the outcast. And this is confusing to his other guests. All the morally upright and religiously respectable people can't relate. "Why is Jesus so connected to these low-lifes?" They think. "Can't he see that they just drag everybody down with them? How is Jesus supposed to get anything done with this rip-raff as his base of support? And why is Jesus so obsessed with the oppressed anyway? They're not important, they're not powerful—often they're abrasive and difficult. It doesn't make any sense."

But again, and again, Jesus makes it very clear—that's just the way it is in God's kingdom. God's ways aren't our ways of upward mobility and efficiency and respectability. God does things differently.

For example, says Jesus, "If you had 100 sheep and one went missing, how many of you would leave the 99 alone while you went looking for the one lost sheep?" Nobody raises their hand. And the people laugh. This is meant to be a joke. No shepherd would do that. It's ridiculous. Why would anyone risk losing 99 good sheep for 1 foolish sheep who's gone off on its own? And yet God loves every single sheep so much that God does strange things for them. God will risk it all for that one errant sheep. Isn't that strange?

Or it's like this, says Jesus, "There's a woman with 10 coins. When she realizes that one is missing, she can't sleep until she's found it again. She tears up her whole house looking for that last coin, and when it finally shows up, she's so excited that she throws a party for all her friends—a party that probably costs more than that lost coin is even worth." Isn't that strange behavior? We might call it obsessive compulsive disorder. Jesus calls it love. He says that in God's community, there's more rejoicing over the one deviant who comes back, than over the 99 who never left. That's just the way it is.

Even though it seems so unfair! Even though the 99 might not like it—not at all.

Just to drive the point home, Jesus then tells a third story—the most famous of all, about a man with two sons. The younger son tells his father to drop dead and then makes off with half their savings only to blow it all in Vegas. After hitting bottom, the kid then wanders back home, thinking he can still at least talk his way into a job at the family business. Only when he gets back the father isn't even mad at him. Instead it turns out the old man has been pining over the boy ever since he left, and when he spots this selfish, entitled child in the distance, the father runs out to embrace him and tells everyone to throw him a party—as if the kid hasn't been partying enough already. Isn't that crazy? No admonishment, no punishment, just a party!

Meanwhile the older son is out in the field, doing his chores, when his father comes out and urges him to come join in the celebration. But the older son isn't having it. He's appropriately indignant. "What gives?" he says to his dad. "That spoiled brat comes traipsing back into town after disowning you and you slaughter a lamb for him—a lamb that technically belongs to me ever since he threw away his part in the business. You're having a party for that miserable excuse for a human being—who has no respect for you, who has no sense whatsoever of his own privilege, who hasn't even really apologized for what he did? Well what about me? While he was off disgracing our family name, I was here working like a slave for you. Taking care of the farm, day after day, year after year. Today you slaughter a lamb for him, but when I wanted to celebrate with my friends, you couldn't even give a ram, Dad! Not even a ram!"

And the thing is—the older brother is right. He's right! Have you ever felt like that? About a sibling or a coworker or somebody in the news who doesn't seem to deserve the treatment they've been getting? I know I have. It seems so unfair. And yet God is like that. God is super obsessed with welcoming back the problematic people, even when they don't deserve it. And the party goes on into the night whether we think it's fair or not. And here's the kicker—God even expects us to join in the celebration too. Like with the older brother in this story, God invites us to come into the party. Isn't that ridiculous? Anybody else besides this crazy father would probably have reacted differently, might have said "what, John is still out working? Well, whatever. If he wants to be like that it's his problem. We got a party going on in here!" Right?

But according to Jesus, it's like the party isn't complete until everybody is invited—everybody! Even the snobbish, self-righteous people who think they're too good to eat with the screw-ups of the world. In the parable, the prodigal father goes out to the field looking for his upstanding son, just like he looked for the other one who had gone astray. And he says to the older one, "Look, buddy, you haven't lost anything, and I haven't forgotten about you—you are still with me, and everything I have left is still yours. But this celebration business—this is who we are. This is what we do in this family. We had to celebrate and rejoice, because this brother of yours was dead and has come to life; he was lost and has been found. So, let's party together, alright?"

I just finished reading this book *Wanted* by Chris Hoke, that I mentioned last month. It took me a long time because it was so good, I wanted to savor it, a little bit at a time. It's a story about men like the younger brother in Jesus' parable. About people whose lives were messed up to the point where society didn't want them anymore. A chaplain meets these unwanted men in jail, starts learning about their stories, tells them about a God who has been out looking for them, calling to them, trying to welcome them back home. And some of these guys, when they hear this message, and experience in relationship what it really feels like to be wanted by somebody—it changes everything for them. It's like a fire is lit within them—a burning desire--a fire that burns away their anger and fear and loneliness. There are stories in here about violent men with tattoos on their faces and necks, now weeping like children, feeling completely overpowered and overwhelmed with the love of God while they lay alone in their isolation cells, hardly believing that this stuff about the kingdom of God could be true—that anyone would care about them, when no one else does. Some of these guys turn their lives around, some don't. Some get out of prison, some just keep going back. Society keeps saying they aren't wanted. God keeps trying to show them that they are, very much, wanted.

Chris writes about this one ex-gang member named Donacio, a guy who finds God in prison and when he gets out starts working for a non-profit in Guatemala City that tries to get other men out of gangs and into legitimate jobs. But then Donacio drops off the radar for a while, so Chris goes looking for him down in Guatemala to see what happened. He figures Donacio has had a relapse or something. But no! Quite the opposite. It turns out that Donacio has just stopped hanging out with the church crowd because he finds the established church to be unwelcoming. Donacio had gotten tired of people treating him and his homies like they weren't wanted after they got out of jail. So, he had gone off on his own and started his own consulting business. As an ex-gang member, he knows how to deal with gangs, so now he hires himself out to bus drivers who are tired of getting held up at gunpoint. Donacio helps them to work things out with the gang-members. And as he does this mediation work, he ends up mentoring a lot of ex-offenders, they come to stay with him and work for him and he is even able to reconcile them with their victims.

So, when Chris visits they're sitting around a table together with a bus driver who has had his leg shot off in a stick up, and a guy who spent years in prison for shooting a bus driver. Donacio points this out to his gringo friend--and he says to him, "The church may not be with us, Chris, but Jesus is with us, bro—and that's all we need."

And he's right. There's no denying it. There in a Guatemalan slum, the lion is laying down with the lamb. There's a table set where wounded people are dining in the presence of their enemies. They now have all things in common, as they break bread together and talk about all the blood that has been shed. Jesus is clearly there with them. Can you see why?

When I read about their communion I think, man I wish the larger church could sit at that table too! I think about how our own disagreements and conflicts would seem like nothing in comparison to what these men have left behind. I wish we all got to be there, joining in that celebration. It's not like that kind of thing can only happen south of the border—we have criminals here in Washington State too, right? But where do you find a church that really wants to hang out with these kinds of people? As in people with serious criminal records and violent tendencies and significant mental health challenges?

Let's say that about 1% of the American population is behind bars—because that's pretty much the rate in this country. Focusing on these people who society has thrown away—it would be like leaving the other 99% in the field—in order to hang out with that 1%. Who would do that, right? It's crazy. It's ridiculous. And yet it's the kingdom of God. It's the Beloved Community. And for some reason Jesus wants you and me to get in on that party. He invites us also to come in and celebrate at that same table. So, what do you think? Are you game?

It's been a while since I asked you to reflect with a neighbor, and this seems like a good time. Because this is one of those hard sayings of Jesus. There's nothing easy about what Jesus is asking of us here. So, I invite you to take a couple minutes to discuss with someone close to you—maybe someone you didn't come to church with today. What's your reaction to Jesus' obsession with outcasts and difficult people? How does it make you feel? What might keep you from joining the party? How do you think we can help each other to get into the celebration? Take a couple minutes just to process your reaction to this crazy invitation of Jesus. If you really must process by yourself, that's okay too—we'll still love you. But either way take a couple minutes and I will call you back with prayer. . .

Toward the Cross
Luke 16

Good morning and welcome back to our journey with Jesus toward the cross through the gospel according to Luke! Today's excerpt is a good one—it's a great story. Like all of Jesus' stories it's beautifully simple and direct, yet so hard to live into. "So high I can't get over it, so low I can't get under it, so wide I can't get around it, gotta go in by the door."

Or in this case, the gate. This is the original story about the pearly gates. Have you ever heard a joke that started out that way? A guy dies and the next thing he knows he's standing before the pearly gates and there's Peter looking at a long list of names. Sound familiar? The pearly gate image is from the book of revelation, and there's no Peter there, but still, that's how it sometimes goes in the Christian imagination.

In the ancient Jewish imagination, though, it was Abraham who met people in stories such as these, because Abraham was the guy known for hospitality—the story went that he would be there welcoming the recently departed into the next life, if there was such a thing. These stories, like the jokes we sometimes tell today, aren't about the afterlife at all—it's just a set up for a punch-line, or to maybe make a point about morality. So, Jesus takes a common fable from the time and uses it to make a point. And to make sure that we get Jesus' point here, I'm going to take this ancient Jewish storyline and update it a bit in my own way. See if anything I add doesn't fit with the original—you can tell me afterwards if you think I missed the point. Sound good?

Oh, and a word about audience. The point of this story is clearly intended for rich people. We know this because the rich man doesn't get a name in the story, meaning that the audience is meant to identify him as another rich person like themselves. So, we also know that Jesus is directing this story at a small group of people, since there weren't many wealthy people in Jesus' day—the society he was talking into in didn't have much of a middle class. There were a few people at the very top who had money and power, and most everyone else was just barely getting by. Scraping by was the normal way of life in ancient Palestine, as it still is for most of the world today. So, if you are just barely scraping by—living pay-check to paycheck, as supposedly 1/3 of Americans do today, then maybe this story isn't so much directed at you. But as for the rest of us, if we have homes and cars and maybe washing machines, it's good to remember that on a global scale, we are very rich indeed, and we are part of this small group Jesus is talking to.

So okay—the story already. Once there was this rich guy, who like most of us, had nice clothes to wear and good food to eat every day. The question on his mind each day wasn't, "Will I have clothes to wear or enough food to eat," but instead he spends a fair amount of time saying to himself, "What shall I wear today? And what am I going to have for dinner?" The man had options. And he was generally a good person, this rich man. He went to church on Sunday and read the bible and knew the commandments of God. The rich man tithed to the church and supported non-profits and donated money to the arts. He had good friends and a healthy family, and all spoke well of him. And the man lived in a well-kept house in the city, with a white picket fence out front.

But on the other side of the rich man's front gate, there was a homeless man named Lazarus who used to lay begging on the sidewalk. Unlike the rich man, Lazarus was not well-kept or well-regarded. In fact, he was not well at all. He had sores all over his body—evidence of some disease that had gone untreated. People assumed Lazarus had gotten sick from his drug use, though no one knows which came first—his homelessness or his coping strategy. What they did know was that Lazarus had a criminal history and that he couldn't seem to hold down a job. And they knew they didn't want anything to do with him.

So, Lazarus didn't get much help there on the street. Lazarus was so hungry most days that he wished he could at least get some scraps from the rich man's table, but he found that the dumpsters were always locked. Like Jesus, Lazarus had no place to lay his head. No place to get out of the weather, not even somewhere to get away from the stray dogs that would come around trying to lick his sores day and night.

Well, as often happens, one day the poor man was gone, and people hardly noticed. He froze to death one night and was picked up by the city in the morning. They cremated the body and labeled the ashes John Doe and disposed of them quietly. But nevertheless, Angels came and carried away Lazarus' spirit to be with Abraham in Heaven.

Meanwhile it was a surprise to everyone when on the very next day, the rich man also died. Of a heart attack. His neighbors thought he would live into his golden years, but not so. When the rich man died, there was an obituary in the paper and a funeral procession in the streets. He had arranged ahead of time for a nice plot in a scenic cemetery, and his family put up a marble headstone to remember him by.

After his death, though, the rich man was surprised to find himself in a place of torment. We might call it hell. It was miserably hot. The rich man was surrounded by flames and he was burning in pain. He looked up and could see Abraham far away in the distance, and Lazarus of all people was there by his side. They seemed to be a in a better place. So, he called out, "Father Abraham! Please, help me! Have mercy on me! Send Lazarus to give me some water to cool my tongue, I'm in agony here."

But Abraham the merciful, Abraham the hospitable couldn't help the rich man. He called back, "Child, remember how blessed you were in your lifetime? How in your privilege you had good things—more than enough to share? But at the same time, it was like Lazarus was cursed. He always seemed to get the short end of the stick. You must have noticed this because he lived right outside your front gate! You must have seen him every day. And yet you did nothing! So now it's the reverse. The lowly have been lifted, and the mighty have been brought low. Now Lazarus is comforted, while you are in agony. This is God's justice. Besides. Even if I wanted to help, I couldn't get to you. Remember that wall you had built to keep Lazarus out of your yard? Here it's more like a great chasm. We can see you, but we can't get to you, and you can't get to us. It's so high we can't get over it, so low we can't go under it. So wide we can't go around it. There's nothing we can do."

The rich man took this in for a minute. The reality of this reversal and of his punishment. If only he had known! If only he had realized. He would have tried to have helped Lazarus while he was alive. He would have invited him to come into his home. He would have done something—anything while he still had the chance. But it was too late!

So, the rich man said to Abraham. "Father Abraham, if this is how it is, then please, I beg you to send Lazarus to warn my family. Have him tell my five brothers so that they won't make the same mistake I did!"

But Abraham replied, "Your family and friends--they already have the scriptures to warn them—the law and the prophets, just like you did. They've heard all of this before--they should pay attention."

The rich man said to him, "But no, Father Abraham—it's not enough! Maybe if someone from here goes to them, they'll change their ways."

Abraham replied, "If they don't listen to the wisdom of the Bible, then they won't be convinced even if someone rises from the dead." And so, the torment of the rich man was that much worse, knowing there was nothing he could do now, for himself or for others—it was too late.

Thus, ends the story of the Rich man and Lazarus, who ended up on opposite sides of the pearly gates. What do you suppose the moral of the story is?

Is it obvious? I think Jesus intended it to be obvious. Jesus didn't have to mention what the law and the prophets said, because he assumed that we who are hearing this story already know the scriptures—as the rich man in the story would have. Scriptures like the story of Abraham in the book of Genesis where Abraham welcomes strangers and feeds them—the rich man clearly knew that one. There are commands throughout the Old Testament law reminding us not to oppress the foreigner or the homeless poor. "There shall be no poor among you." Says Deuteronomy 15:4. Or how about this verse from the prophet Isaiah: "Isn't this the fast I choose, says the Lord, sharing your bread with the hungry and bringing the homeless poor into your house, covering the naked when you see them." Jesus told his disciples, when you do these things to others, you do them to me!

And yet like the man in this story, we sometimes miss these scriptures that are a central part of our bible, or we pretend they aren't there. Just like the homeless people in our city who we slowly cease to notice—the people in need who get pushed further and further away from our awareness through city codes that outlaw panhandling or camping or sleeping on park benches. As a society, we erect fences—sometimes invisible barriers to employment or housing, other times physical restraints in the form of prison bars and border walls. Sometimes we throw up our hands and say, "It's not our fault, we didn't build the walls!" But then Jesus, in ways sometimes subtle, and sometimes quite blunt, says to us, "Maybe so, but you still have access to the gate! Maybe it's time you used it. You can still cross over to where Lazarus is, or better yet, help him to come in—while there's still time."

Part of me wants to soften this story of Jesus today. Because I'm a rich man, and I've got all the excuses that rich men and women use to justify our privilege. But to make excuses for the economic disparities that we Americans participate in would be dishonoring to Jesus—our savior and Lord who lived like Lazarus, and then died, and then came back from the dead in order to warn us. Jesus came to tell us again that it's not too late to choose the way of compassion. Jesus said he can even empower us to do it. There's another time in the gospels, Jesus is talking to his disciples and he says to us, "I am the gate! I am the way to the other side of that wall. It may seem impossible to get there, but with God, all things are possible for those who believe." Jesus says "I can help you cross over—if you'll just follow me. If you'll just listen to me and trust me." Can we do that together, while we still have time?

I invite you to reflect on what it would look like for you, personally, to cross through that gate and connect with Lazarus this week. It doesn't have to be anything radical or dramatic, though that would be fine too—since Jesus sometimes calls us to radical and dramatic change. But what if it was something small? Remember that quote from Mother Theresa— "There are no great deeds, only small deeds done with great love?" We can start small. "Small is beautiful"—as Ghandi used to say. Both Mother Theresa and Ghandi benefited from hanging out with poor people. Rev James Forbes used to say, in keeping with this story, "Nobody gets to heaven without a letter of reference from the poor." So, I ask you this morning, who's your poor person that's' going to help you get into heaven? It doesn't hurt to have more than one. When I'm applying for a job, I don't just look for one reference. The more the better, right?! And it's good if those references are recent—a decade ago doesn't count. So, who would you ask to recommend you to the almighty? Again, often it doesn't take much—there's a non-profit in Seattle called "Facing Homelessness" that wants people to simply build personal relationships with the homeless poor—to put a face on the issue of homelessness, to humanize it. Their slogan is "just say hello." I try to remember this when I drive by a panhandler—that the least I can do is smile and wave. And yet this alone is so hard to do. Because if I wave, then I feel bad for not stopping or giving something to help like a pair of socks. But even a smile is better than nothing, right? Ideally, I'd want to know the names of the people who are outside my front gate, so to speak. Like when I lived in Chicago, I would drive my bike past this guy who stood on the side of the road trying to wash people's windows. I learned his name was Omar, and every time I'd ride or drive past him, I'd wave and say Hey, Omar! And he'd smile, and it seemed like it made his day. Reading this story of Jesus, I'm reminded that kind of thing also isn't enough. Even the rich guy in Jesus' story knew Lazarus' name—it wasn't enough. So, I wish I could have taken Omar home with me. I wish we could make space here for more than just 5 or 6 family's downstairs at Julia's Place. I wish Terrence, the guy who has sometimes stayed on our back porch here in the winter time--I wish I could help him to get clean and get indoors. I wish we had more tiny houses to help people like the woman who's staying with Keith Preece up in Lynwood. Keith explained to me a couple weeks ago how her trailer park burned down, and she's been couch surfing ever since. But where will she go when Keith dies of cancer? It kills me that we don't have the ability to help these people who have been dealt a bad hand in life. People who are every bit as deserving as we are. People who sometimes simply need a break, a second chance, the makings for basic human dignity.

It kills me to feel so helpless to provide for these people I meet. And yet isn't that maybe part of what Jesus intends for us? To feel the pain of our neighbors—the pain of people like Lazarus? To care enough that we find ourselves on their side of the fence? So that we can share with them, both in blessings and in burdens, so that at some point it no longer feels like us and them, but our life together in the Beloved Community trying to figure out together how to live lives of mutual care and support?

If you know what I'm talking about, if you also feel this way, then take heart. For God is here with us, working on this very issue. Jesus is here, in the form of Lazarus, sharing in the pain that we feel for those who are suffering. And we can take heart knowing that whether we are rich or poor, we have access to the God of all compassion, who does not abandon us to suffering or to indifference but seeks to lead us to places of comfort and hope and connection, together. Saying to us again and again, now is the time to reach out, to cross through that gate. Today is the day to make that phone call, to strike up a conversation, to schedule your appointment, to use the blessings we've been given to bless others, to change our stories, to find our way into life and life to its full. It's not too late, not for us, not for you. But it could be too late tomorrow. Today is the day of salvation—and we must seize it! We have to love as though our lives depend on it. Because if very well might. It very well might. Amen?

The Sheep and the Goats
Matt 25:31-46

I don't know about you, but this scripture used to scare the bejeebers out of me. Is that a word, bejeebers? Mostly when I was young, I was concerned about this judgment language that Jesus uses in the Gospel of Matthew--the whole weeping and gnashing of teeth thing. It didn't seem fair to me how Jesus separated the sheep from the goats and then told the goats to take a flying leap. What's wrong with goats? They're just as cute as sheep! And they seem much more intelligent.

I remember when I was in middle school, I went through confirmation class at my church and became a member of the church, and then I decided I should read through the bible, so that I'd know what I'd signed up for. And I knew enough to start with the New Testament, since the Old Testament has some dry sections that can be discouraging to early readers. So, Matthew came first. And I was really enjoying it. The Sermon on the Mount made a lot of sense to my junior-high self. It was good news to hear that I didn't need to worry about stuff--what I was going to eat, what I was going to wear. God would take care of me. Awesome. I could understand that, since my parents took care of my food and clothing. Check! And then I read all these parables about the Kingdom of God--how just and loving and peaceable life will be when Jesus is in charge. I totally wanted in on that. Sign me up for the wedding banquet--I'm going to buy that field, I'm not going to miss out on that party. Ain't no party like a holy ghost party, cause the Holy Ghost Party don't stop!

But then I got to this section about the end times, when Jesus talks about what will happen when the kingdom is on its way to coming in full, and he says not everybody is going to make the cut. And suddenly, I was a little concerned. I felt like I did sometimes in gym class when they were picking teams for soccer, going down the line saying, John's going to be on team A, and Ryan's going to be on team B, and I suddenly realized that I might not get picked for the right team. I wanted to be on Jesus' team! I realized that I didn't want to be a goat! Not that being a goat is all ba-a-ad, they make good milk, but I wanted to be a sheep, so I could hang out with Jesus. The guy who seems to want everybody on his team, because he's nice like that. I want to be on the team where all the little kids get to play, and it doesn't matter if you're not all that good of a player, because the goal isn't to win anything, but to enjoy the game. To glorify God and enjoy God forever. That's what Jesus' team is all about. That would be enough to make all the running around worthwhile. Jesus has a way of making life joyful. That's why I wanted to put on the sheepskin jersey.

So, imagine my dismay when I read this section about judgment where Jesus says that some people won't make it. And the goats won't even know they're goats until it's too late. I remember sitting on my bed at home with my bible on my lap as I read this, picturing all the people in my church who could be thinking they were sheep, and really, they were goats. What if my parents were goats? What if I was a goat already!! In fact, according to this criterion, I most certainly had to be a goat, after all, I was only 12 years old. When had I ever fed the hungry or taken care of a sick person, or visited anyone in prison? What if in the end, Jesus came to me and said to me, "Just as you did NOT do it to one of the least of these, you did NOT do it to me." I would be devastated.

In the years since I first read this passage, I've heard a lot of explanations for Jesus' words that soften his criteria a little bit. We could say, for instance, that since we're all a part of the body of Christ at work in the world--we are all different body parts with different functions, then maybe we don't all have to be concerned about each of these six acts of mercy that Jesus mentions. Maybe I'm just supposed to help support the people who are doing the feeding and visiting and welcoming, etc.--I don't necessarily have to do it myself, personally. And that's possible. Though Jesus does seem to be talking about individuals here. He doesn't say "as you all" did it to one of the least of these," Jesus says, "as you, Mark, did to one of the least of these." --there's some personal responsibility here.

But then again, he doesn't necessarily say we have to do all the acts of mercy either, maybe I can specialize in clothing the naked, while other people worry about the cooking and the giving of water. Then, in my defense, I can at least say I did something to help someone in need. Right? But what I struggled with as a young person, was "What if that's not enough?" What if Jesus still points out the times, I missed someone. Like the countless times I have walked past a homeless person without stopping, or when I've seen hungry people on TV but not sent money, or when I've known someone was in the hospital, but just didn't get there in time to visit. Those words of Jesus are so haunting--"just as you did not do for one of the least off these, you did not do it to me." It's enough to give you a pretty bad guilt trip.

I remember being so concerned about this possibility of judgement, that it almost kept me up at night. All the what-ifs. What if in the end it's not good enough, I'm not good enough? Will I miss out on the kingdom? So, I went to talk to my youth pastor at the time--I'm grateful now that there was such a thing--it was helpful to have Bruce to talk to, and I know now that he probably found my questions energizing also. We did some bible study together and Bruce tried to assure me that Jesus didn't say these things to scare people--at least not entirely, Bruce said to me, "Mark, Jesus doesn't want us to live our lives in fear. We'll meet Jesus face-to-face someday, and it's true we'll be accountable for our actions or lack of action--but he's also here, now, and you can talk to him about this whole sheep/goat issue if it's bothering you."

So, I did. I prayed to Jesus to help make me a sheep rather than a goat. "God," I said, "help me out here. I don't know anybody who's hungry or thirsty or naked. But you are the great shepherd, and I want to follow you into your kingdom--so I'll do my best--I'll try, and I hope it will be enough. Jesus, remember me, when you come into your kingdom."

I prayed this way from time to time that year, though unfortunately my fear of judgment didn't go away immediately. Months later my youth pastor Bruce moved on from the church for some reason, and I was sad not to have anyone to talk to about this anymore. But then one day I got a letter in the mail (snail mail--this was before the internet, you see) and this is what Bruce wrote to me. "Dear Mark," he said, "Forget about this whole sheep and goat business. You're in. Period. You are a beloved Child of God and nothing will ever change that. So, stop worrying about it. Yours in Christ, Bruce."

That was it--very simple and to the point. And the miracle was that I believed it. Right then and there. There were no tears or anything, I think I kind of laughed about it. "Oh, right--I'm in. Duh." And that was that. Something about having someone say it directly--maybe seeing it in black-and-white, it suddenly made sense.

Of course, Jesus doesn't want us to live in fear of judgment--he tells this story yet another example of what it means to live in the kingdom of God--serving the least of God's children is what we're supposed to do because we are already a part of God's Beloved community, it's not a criterion for getting in. We've already made the cut. That's why Jesus is telling us where to look for him, where we will find him. This form of service is how we get to experience life, and life to its full, through feeding and visiting and clothing and welcoming. This is the key to the kingdom, and we already have it--because we have Jesus, the center of the Beloved Community, the King of the kingdom!

And I'll never forget that letter from Bruce, because it changed my life. There was something really empowering about this declaration for me--this discovery, that indeed, I'm already in. It doesn't make for much of a story, but I wanted to share it with you because it made such a big difference in my life and I believe it can make a big difference in the life of others, as they also discover the joy of this good news. When I realized that I was already a part of God's kingdom--that indeed I had already been baptized into Christ's resurrected life and claimed as one of his sheep forever--then I was free to stop worrying about my salvation and start enjoying the party. After that I signed up for every service opportunity I could at my church, because I read in scripture that I could meet Jesus there. Sure, I could encounter him also in the breaking of the bread, in the teaching of the apostles, in prayer. But I soon discovered that when I felt most alive, was when I had the opportunity to spend time with the least of these--children, homeless people, poor people in other countries. It wasn't until I was older that I got opportunities to visit sick people and welcome strangers, and it still hasn't worked out for me to get set up for visiting prisoners--there's a lot of red tape around that one. But I'm excited about that too, because I know from this letter, that that's where Jesus hangs out--behind barbed wire like the picture of Jesus that hangs in my office that's also on your bulletin today. And this Jesus, my friends, is the King of the kingdom--the one who makes real life possible. He is the great shepherd who cares for all us--cares so much for us that he's even willing to scare us a little bit from time to time in order to point us in the right direction.

I have a greater appreciation for this tactic now that I have children my own. Last week, for instance, I was picking up my two-year-old son, Caleb, from his babysitter's house, and it was raining outside, and Caleb didn't want to put on his coat. He has very particular preferences about clothing these days and I think maybe that coat is too bulky for him, but it was all we had that day, and he had just gotten over a cold, and I wasn't going to let him go out without his coat, so after wrestling for a couple minutes I got down low to reason with him. I looked him straight in the eyes and I said to him, real serious like, "Caleb, you have to wear your coat when it is raining, you know why? Because if you don't wear your coat you're going to get all wet and cold and you'll be shivering and you'll be shaking so bad that you'll lose your balance and go bonk on the sidewalk and you'll be crying and sad and have an owie, and then you'll get sick like you were last week with all that horrific snot, and I'll have to wipe your nose constantly, so much that it will get raw and bloody and you will be weeping and gnashing your teeth!"

Caleb said "Okay."

And the babysitter said, "Oh my gosh, Mark, he's never going to take off his coat again!"

So maybe I overdid it, but he put his coat on that day, and hopefully he got the point. And my point is also this. Was it a serious threat? No! Obviously, I wasn't going to let any of those bad things happen--why? Because Caleb is my son, whom I love, and I'm going to protect him as best I can. There will come a day--maybe when he goes off to college, when I won't be there to remind him to put on his coat, and if he hasn't learned by then how to clothe himself, then there might be some weeping and gnashing of teeth. Or he'll just move to a dryer climate, who knows. But I hope he learns to just put the coat on.

And that's what Jesus is calling us to do also in today's scripture passage. To clothe ourselves with righteousness and justice. To remember that if we want to live in his kingdom--both today, and into the distant future, we've got to be people of compassion who dedicate ourselves to serving the least of God's children. And this isn't a heavy obligation. We can do this with joy, knowing that if this is where Jesus shows up, then it is in these acts of mercy--feeding, clothing, visiting, welcoming, this is where true life is found. This is where we discover faith, hope, and love. This is where we find true community--Beloved Community. This is how we experience the gifts of the Holy Spirit--love, joy, peace, patience, kindness, gentleness, faithfulness, self-control. All we must do is serve. Not because we'll be damned if we don't, but because Jesus, our King, is among us as one who serves, and promises us there is life in this service. We serve the least of these because we are blessed to be in relationship with this one who loves us so much that he himself lived and died as the least of these, and now he reigns on high, in order that we also might have life, and life to its full.

At Last
John 2:1-11

This morning, being MLK weekend I want to talk a little bit about that great prophet of the 20th century, the Rev. Dr Martin Luther King Jr. These days we get to revere Dr King as the public figure for whom our King county is named. We love him and miss him as the preacher who popularized the term The Beloved Community that is so central to our mission here at Madrona Grace Presbyterian Church. We get to remember and celebrate today the gift of the dream Dr King instilled in our collective consciousness—the vision of a society in which all people would come together to overcome the evils or racism, militarism, and materialism. We shall overcome! Dr King gave us hope.

But here our church at least, we also remember that Dr King's hope didn't start with him and wasn't even grounded or centered in Martin King—his personality or ideology. Rev. Dr King was simply preaching the good news given to him by Jesus. Martin Luther King Jr. was first and foremost a person of faith, who helped us to see God at work in the world. He taught us how to seek first the kingdom of God and God's righteousness—the righteousness of non-violent love that turns enemies into friends and brings about true justice and peace for all God's children. That was his gospel as well as ours.

So, when we talk about Dr King, we should also always talk about Jesus, and begin with these stories of scripture that were so formative for Dr King, that made him who he was and made up the content of his message to us. But I must acknowledge that unfortunately this can sometimes be challenging to do—to keep focused on Jesus, to keep reading and learning from scripture, because our society isn't as friendly toward faith as it used to be.

This April will mark the 50th anniversary of the assassination of Martin Luther King Jr. 1968-2018. It's been 50 years since he was taken from us. 50 years. He was 39 then, He'd be 89 years old tomorrow. Can you believe that? The world has changed a great deal in 50 years, I wonder what he would think of all that has taken place. How would he have dealt with things like Mass incarceration, Global warming, or Donald Trump? It's a different world today and in many ways, worse. The church has declined in numbers and influence—particularly denominations like ours. And a lot of people even celebrate that decline. When you watch the movie Spotlight and learn how the Catholic Church protected child molesters, or when you hear on the news how Evangelical Christians today continue to support Roy Moore while ignoring those women who he abused. A lot of people—particularly the younger generations—are understandably opting out of organized religion. They're saying, if that's what Christianity is, then I want nothing to do with it. And it's hard to blame them for feeling this way.

I feel that tension even with today's scripture passage—the story of Jesus turning water into wine. With all the things going on today, this miracle feels a little out of touch. Elsewhere people may be talking about the fate of the DACA Dreamers or what's going to happen with this border wall, and in church we're going to talk about Jesus making more wine so that a bunch of people can continue to get drunk at a wedding. It comes across as a little trivial even, this first miracle in the Gospel of John, don't you think? It brings up images of rich people bringing out ever more expensive bottles of wine to enjoy amongst themselves, while outside there are homeless people struggling to stay warm and dry. We know there are people in Detroit and Puerto Rico struggling to find clean drinking water. And yet Jesus is drinking wine?

No wonder Christians sometimes disparage this fourth gospel for being a bit too otherworldly. Too heavenly minded to be any earthly good. In the synoptic gospels Jesus at least leads with activities that seem a bit more relevant. In Matthew Jesus starts out with the sermon on the mount—blessed are the poor, he says. Don't return evil for evil, says Jesus. Revolutionary stuff. In the gospel of Mark Jesus begins his ministry by casting out a demon. We can work with that too. Let's cast out the evils of domination, the exploitation of empire! Likewise, in the gospel of Luke Jesus announces in the synagogue his mission to free the prisoners and proclaim jubilee. Freedom from poverty. Freedom from oppression. Love that! But then we get to John's gospel, and after calling his disciples we find Jesus reclining at a wedding reception listening to people complain about the lack of wine. What's with that?

I imagine therefore many people in the movement for justice today assume that religion is no longer relevant. Maybe it was helpful 50 or 100 years ago as a starting point, but now we've come to the end and it has nothing more to teach us. They assume the tradition is bankrupt and it's time to move on. This might explain why so few millennials go to church. It's an understandable perspective. It is.

And yet I don't think Dr. King would agree with this. Do you? I don't think he would have given up on John's gospel. And not just because he was of a different generation. I think Rev. King would stick with it because he was an educated man—a scholar as well as an activist who understood that you often must look beneath the surface in order to grasp the meaning of a story. Whether that be the story of a human being—looking beyond one's skin color, or in scripture--looking for the context behind the text. It's not just the literal word, but the symbolic word—that's what John's gospel is all about.

So, I checked out this story of Jesus turning the water into wine. I investigated the context, as I know Dr. King would have, and it changed my perspective a little bit. Here's how I read it now. Listen again to the story of the water and the wine:

Jesus and his disciples are at a wedding. They have an important mission to accomplish in the world, but at the same time they aren't too serious or self-important as to neglect the common celebrations of life. We must celebrate the little things, even during the struggle. Amen? A politician might have declined this wedding invitation, but Jesus—he shows up whenever we invite him to. All we must do is ask. If we think it's important, then it's important to Jesus. Because Jesus cares about people. He cares about us. He doesn't just care about a cause or an ideal. Jesus loves US just as we are. Oh, and Jesus loves his mom too. He might have gone to that wedding just because his mom asked him to. Because the work of justice doesn't give us an excuse to neglect our parents. You with me?

So, Jesus goes to a wedding out in this random town called Cana. That's Cana as in the Cana-nites. If you know the old testament, you know that's a reference to an ancient enemy of Jesus' people. There's an old grudge there. This might be a Jewish wedding they're attending, but it's still in enemy territory, among foreign people, on the other side of the tracks, on the other side of the isle so to speak. But Jesus has no problem with that. Because Jesus is a person of reconciliation in the midst of his justice work. If only Republicans and Democrats would go to each other's weddings today.

Anyway, that's only part of the back-story. Turns out that in Jesus' time this town of Cana was near the worship site of a popular deity known for throwing raucous parties—the god of wine. Dionisius, for those who know Greek mythology. So now Jesus has now taken his disciples to a morally questionable wedding, with idolatrous connections to alcohol. And what's the next thing that happens?

His mom turns to him and says, "Jesus, they're out of wine!" Crazy, right? This would have been shocking to everybody involved. Not totally different from how people might react today if they ran out of wine at a modern wedding, only a little worse on account of the back-story. I mean, "What do you mean they're out of wine—this is the city of wine! How can you be in

Napa and not find a vineyard? These people worship the god of wine!" So, what does it mean? Is the celebration over, are the people bankrupt, is there nothing left? It's a scandalous problem.

And yet worse than that, it's embarrassing for the guests too. Because apparently in that culture, weddings were BYOB. Bring your own bottle to share. Realistically, rich people probably brought a lot of wine, poor people like Jesus and his disciples might not have brought any at all, but the responsibility for the wine fell to the guests, not the bridal party. So, when they run out of wine, it's a commentary on how poor the guests are at this wedding. These people are so down and out that they can't even afford to celebrate a wedding properly. How sad is that? This is surely the end. They've hit rock bottom. So, Jesus' Mother is understandably upset. She says to Jesus pointedly, "They are out of wine!"

And Jesus responds to her with the same indifference that we have when we first read this story. Yeah, they're out of wine--so what! What's that got to do with me? Can't you see we have more important problems do deal with these days?" Jesus responds this way too, during the party. I find it validating that even Jesus can come across as a bit snarky sometimes. And yet without skipping a beat, Jesus then goes ahead and helps them out anyway. Even though in the larger scheme of things it seems like a trivial request, God answers the prayers of the people anyway. Isn't that something? Ask, seek, knock—Jesus responds to those he loves.

They ask him, indirectly, for just a little bit more wine. And lo and behold, Jesus gives them even more than they ask for. He doesn't just find another couple bottles, Jesus responds with a full-blown, miraculous amount of wine. Because that's the way God is with God's children. Jesus says, "you want some wine, I'll show you some wine. You see those giant jars of water over there—the ones they use for ritual purification. We're going to take that old ritual and make something completely new out of it. We're going to take that old, stale water that people have been wringing their hands in for days, and we're going to make of it a new creation, a better creation. More abundant and beautiful than anything these wine worshiping people could even imagine.

So, the people do what Jesus instructs them to do, they draw a bit of water from those old containers, they bring it to the guy in charge of the bar, and that wine steward tastes the new wine and begins to smile. He grabs the mike and announces with amazement, "I can't believe it, everybody. The host saved the best for last! We thought we were all out, that there was nothing left here worth anything, but the one who brought us all together saved the best for last. The party isn't over—the best is yet to come!"

That was Jesus' first miracle—that was it--water into wine. And the irony is that it was his first miracle, but it wasn't the last time he did it. There came a day much later, when Jesus' own people were done with HIM. They figured Jesus had nothing left to teach and was just getting in the way, so they strung him up and nailed him to a cross. This time they offered him some very old wine—wine gone bad, to at least ease the pain of death. But he refused to drink it, because Jesus isn't into old wine. "It is finished" he said. And they thought that Jesus was done. End of story. But then three days later, again it turned out that the story wasn't over. It was only just beginning. And ever since people have been noticing this sign—all over the world, wine being taken and blessed and shared. And amazingly the wine seems to get better rather than worse. Isn't that amazing? We haven't run out yet. God has indeed saved the best for last!

Since Dr King's death in 1968 there have been many who have said that the movement for justice is over. That the legacy of Rev. Dr. King is gone. They've even said that the voice of the church is over, done, bankrupt. But we believe in a God who can make wine out of water! We follow a savior who is all about taking old things and making them new. We still worship this same Jesus who comes back again and again and again, to answer the prayers of broken, oppressed people. Particularly when it seems least likely. When the night is darkest, and it feels as though all hope has been lost. That's when our God likes to make a move.

Dr King knew this. That's why 50 years ago he was working on the poor people's campaign. Because Rev. King knew that God likes to help poor people, since they are often the ones with the least power and the least hope—the most in need of new wine. So, I believe Rev King would have a great deal of hope for the world today. Because there are a great number of poor people in our midst today. And God's going to make some wine out of that water.

People may talk negatively about this younger generation—the millennials. That they're not capable of anything more than hashtag activism or enlightened consumerism. They can't seek justice because they're too busy posting selfies while sipping their lattes. These millennials are described as lazy, entitled, hopelessly ego-centric. How are they going to put together a movement like the boomers did? They may be bigger than any previous generation, but they're nothing like the greatest generation—they've never sacrificed for their country, let alone for a cause.

And yet who are these people really, these young people of the same age as Martin Luther King? They're also the first generation of Americans to fare worse economically than their parents. They're people who came of age during the longest consecutive wars in American history. They're a generation that entered the workforce during the worst economic downturn since the great depression. Some of them may be entitled, sure. But what's truer about them as a generation is that they're poor. And traumatized. Grappling with the reality of corporate rule and ecological devastation, mass incarceration and mass extinctions—oh and the threat of nuclear holocaust. These Millennials may be slaves to their smartphones, but don't let that fool you. Because what is it that God does with slaves? What does scripture tell us that God does with oppressed people, forgotten people, those who are left out and the left behind?

Dr King knew, as we learn in scripture, that there is power in poor people. So, say that. Say out loud "there's power in poor people." **There's power in poor people.** And Dr King was working on the poor people's campaign because he saw a wedding coming. A powerful wedding. A wedding of black people and white people. Indigenous people and Spanish speaking people. Even Democrats and Republicans (lord help us!) they're all coming to this wedding. It'll take a miracle for everyone to get along, but there's a wedding coming. So, turn to your neighbor, and tell them, there's a wedding coming! **There's a wedding coming!**

Friends there's a wedding coming, with wine and dancing and justice for all. It's going to happen because the movement is not over. The fire has not gone out. There is a new campaign being planned to continue what Rev. Dr. King started, and the new wine is going to be even better than the old. So, turn to your neighbor, tell them, there's a wedding coming, and we're all invited. **There's a wedding coming, and we're all invited**.

God knows people may feel worn out and too tired for a wedding. Too spent for a celebration. Many don't believe it's possible. What can all these poor people do anyway? If Bill Gates and Barack Obama and Warren Buffet and Oprah Winfrey, if these rich people haven't been able to fix it our economy yet, what hope to we have? But never forget that God likes to save the best for last! The first shall be last and the last shall be first. There are still new things to be done. More justice to come! Say it, God has saved the best for last! **God has saved the best for last!**

It's a celebration, friends! Because there's going to be justice in this world AT LAST. There's going to be love between our brothers and our sisters. At Last. Trump says make America great again. But Jesus says those water jars were never great to begin with, so let's take them and make them into something new. Let's make America Great AT LAST!

At last God's people will be free of fear. At last we will be free of discrimination and hatred. At last we will be free to love again. Free to be the people God made us to be, a new creation, made one in the one who died and rose again in order to take the common water of our lives, and transform it into wine. The very best wine. AT LAST. Thank God almighty that we will be free AT LAST!

I'm going to end with these words of Dr King from the last sermon he gave before his death. Hear these words as the beginning of a new chapter in God's movement toward the Beloved Community. Because in 2018 it's time not just to commemorate Dr. King's work, but to get it working again, Amen?

"I think it is necessary for us to realize that we have moved from the era of civil rights to the era of human rights…[W]hen we see that there must be a radical redistribution of economic and political power, then we see that for the last twelve years we have been in a reform movement…That after Selma and the Voting Rights Bill, we moved into a new era, which must be an era of revolution…In short, we have moved into an era where we are called upon to raise certain basic questions about the whole society."

Washing Feet
John 13:1-17

Today's gospel story from the book of John is partially about service, so I'm going to focus on this theme of service today, even though I think it's a theme that maybe gets overdone sometimes, to the point where we can take it for granted. By that I mean that in some ways service as a value has gone mainstream in our society. I'm thinking of corporate trainings that focus on serving the needs of customers. Putting service first—that kind of thing. In professional leadership circles they talk about "servant leadership" or "leadership as service" But without a reference to Jesus, this can become just a commonly understood way of getting ahead—service can be a way to network, to build one's personal brand, to win friends and influence people. And then there's the whole "Service Industry"—one of the fastest growing segments of our economy that has become a way of getting paid to serve other people. So, we might not all mean the same things when we talk about "service" as a concept.

But in this story Jesus doesn't just talk about service—he models it—Jesus often has a way of putting flesh on things that really gets to the heart of service in way that is a little more challenging than what most motivational speakers might be saying. So, it's helpful that in church we get called back to this simple story again and again and again—the story of Jesus washing the disciples' feet is central to the gospel.

I remember one time I personally experienced this story in a concrete way. When I was a young adult, near the end of college, I had a good relationship with my Pastor at the time—a very humble man named Ken. And at some point, I think he got the sense that I was a little entitled, as young adults can often be. I loved the little church we were a part of, but I was new there and hadn't gotten involved to the point of contributing much to the community. Looking back, I don't think that I knew how to contribute—I didn't know what my gifts were, didn't know what the community needed. I was shy, and I didn't know how long I would be able to stick around. I had lots of excuses for holding back.

Well Ken saw this, and maybe he tried talking to me about it, but when I didn't understand what he was getting at, he tried something unique with me—somewhat of an object lesson. This is something that I don't know if I would ever be bold enough or crazy enough to try, so I give him kudos for taking a risk. Here's what happened.

Ken invited a group of us from the church to his small studio apartment on Capitol hill for a Saturday brunch. It was just a fellowship gathering. I didn't know the other people all that well, so I figured it was a good opportunity to build some relationships. And I knew the food would be good since Ken had owned a restaurant at one point earlier in life. Well I got there, and the room was cramped with the dozen or so people in his 500 square feet. Ken didn't have much furniture, and I ended up claiming a small space on the edge of the bed where I felt like I wouldn't be in the way. I tried to make casual conversation with the person next to me as we were all kind of waiting for the food to get passed out of Ken's tiny little one-person kitchen. And as the food came out, an odd thing happened. Ken brought some plates directly to me where I was sitting on his bed, and suddenly, he got down on his knees right in front of me and started handing me things one at a time. A napkin, a cup that he filled up with orange juice. He asked me if I'd like some syrup with my pancakes. Then he poured it for me. "Is there anything else I can get you?" he asked, oh so innocently. Of course, everyone in this studio apartment was starting at us awkwardly. And I felt incredibly embarrassed. I said, "Ken, what are you doing? Please, stop." But he just kept going, making a show of serving me hand and foot. I continued to protest, and he said, "are you sure? Do you understand?" And I said, "Yes, yes—for goodness sake, enough already!" Ken didn't have to keep going. I got the point. I got it. It was embarrassing—humiliating even, being served that way. And it's an experience that I've never forgotten. Of course, I realized immediately that Ken was just imitating Jesus—that's exactly what Jesus does here in this story with his disciples. So now I understand what they must have been feeling. I bet these first disciples never forgot this food-washing incident either.

They and we would continue to remember how Jesus, on that night of the Passover, didn't just serve dinner to his friends, he insisted on taking off their sandals and washing their feet. Which first of all would have been super stinky and dirty in that poor community where feet were exposed, and outhouses were hard to come by. And second, this was a job which at the time was reserved for people of the lowest possible status—particularly slaves, and apparently only female slaves. So, for Jesus to take on this role of washing their feet would have been humiliating—not just for him, but for the guys who let him do it. Jesus was breaking all sorts of norms in this action—hierarchy, patriarchy, basic social convention. Peter, who was probably the oldest of Jesus' first 12 disciples, was so scandalized and appalled that at first, he refused to go along with it. Essentially saying, "Jesus, this is really embarrassing. You can make your point some other way—you're never going to wash my feet, that would be inappropriate. It's beneath you!" But Jesus insisted. He said, if you don't let me wash your feet, then you have no part in me." Why? Because it wasn't just an ideological point Jesus was making.

Jesus wasn't just giving the disciples a seminar on servant leadership. Jesus was trying to help them to see that real service means getting down and dirty with people. Like spitting in mud and putting it in people's eyes. Like lifting sick people up. Cleaning toilets. Listening to painful stories. Getting stripped and beaten and hung out to dry. That's the kind of service and vulnerability Jesus models for us. He does it for us, so that we'll do it for others. Not just in theory, but in the flesh.

Well, rather than being kicked out of the dinner party, Peter of course tells Jesus he can wash his feet, uncomfortable as that is. "If that's what it takes," says Peter, then not just my feet, but my hands and my head as well." Only then we find out that Jesus doesn't want his disciples to get into dependency mode either. He only washes their feet—he says the rest of them are clean already.

And it's is an interesting balance Jesus strikes in this scene, don't you think? Only the feet—that's enough. Have you noticed how often our tendency when it comes to service is all or nothing? Either we refuse to get involved at all, or when we do serve somebody, we then feel obligated to do everything for that person. But Jesus doesn't go to either of those extremes. He gets involved—he serves, physically, concretely, but he doesn't go overboard and become a doormat either. Jesus still has boundaries. The idea is to serve and be served, not to become a slave or a master. It's mutuality in contrast to hierarchy or dependency.

This is the kind of balance I continue to struggle with when I contemplate our call to service these days. It can be difficult discernment—knowing when we may be acting entitled and when we are maybe enabling others to continue with a sense of entitlement. How do you know when enough is enough?

So fortunately, Jesus has more to say to us about this. He says to the disciples, and to us, "Since I've washed your feet, you should wash one another's feet. I've set an example so that you should do what I've done for you." Again, it's a call to mutuality—wash one another's feet. Not just some people washing, and other people getting washed. It must go both ways. There's got to be mutuality in service, otherwise it creates hierarchy and domination, which Jesus came to undo. That's one good goal for service—mutuality.

It's good to return to this teaching of Jesus because it's so counter-cultural these days. Despite all the talk about service, the reality is that most people hope to graduate out of it someday. They might be forced to serve early on in their career, but then some day they aspire to be in charge so that they can sit back while other people will serve them. Can you imagine a society in which that wasn't the expectation? Can you imagine instead a world in which all people were expected to serve and be served at the same time? As if all people were capable and worthy of both actions?

It's been interesting to me observing the rise of the Trump administration and its attack on government services. The prevailing attitude seems to be one of entitlement, in which rich people deserve what they have and shouldn't be obligated to support programs for poor people. Likewise, the government shouldn't be serving to protect the environment or the rights of workers or the safety of immigrants. And "America First" means that we don't serve our global neighbors either. This isolationist attitude assumes that we don't really need our neighbors—as if they don't already serve our best interests in a variety of ways.

Isn't that frustrating? I feel so angry when I hear Trump quote scripture and use Christian language even though his actions are the opposite of the love and service that Jesus modeled for us. Can you imagine anyone in that administration getting down on the floor and washing someone's feet?

And yet here's where this foot washing story of Jesus continues to convict me. No matter how many times I come back to it, it's still uncomfortable. Because notice also how Jesus' washes all the disciples' feet. All of them. Even the ones he knows will soon betray him. He serves Judas, even though he knows that Judas is going to reject this model of service and walk out on him. Part of me wants to say, "No, Jesus, you can wash my feet—I'll gladly wash yours, but don't wash Judas' feet. He's not worth it—Judas is selfish, he's entitled, he's not one of us!"

And yet this is Jesus' way of saving the world through service. Jesus even washes the feet of his enemies. And in the process, he doesn't scold them or demand that they change. He simply washes their feet. And then Jesus goes to the cross. Jesus lays down his life, he faces death, willingly. For them! Not just for us, but for the whole world. For the selfish ones, and the servile ones, and everyone in-between. Whether they become people of mutual service or not. That's what's radical and powerful about this way of Jesus. Jesus loves the world to death, and then invites us to go and do likewise. Can you believe that?

I don't know about you, but I sometimes still have a hard time with it. That Jesus expects us to love people to death—whether they deserve it or not. It's a tough teaching. I mean, I don't want to die. I don't want to betrayed or humiliated either. Service is one thing, but caring for entitled people? That really pushes my buttons.

And yet this is what Jesus does for us. We who sometimes think that we've got it all figured out. We who are sometimes quick to judge and slow to forgive. We who sometimes feel like we've put in our time and now it's someone else's turn. Still, Jesus goes to the cross for us also. Even when we don't deserve it. Even when we resist and protest his call to service, Jesus kneels in front of us, takes off our shoes, and smells our stinky feet. Do we still want to go this way? Are we willing to go there with Jesus?

Friends, I don't know if I've ever mentioned to you one of the reasons, I'm still here in the church trying to stay faithful to this path of service. One reason I keep coming back is that I've been blessed with so many great examples of servants like Jesus throughout my life. And with few exceptions they've all been Christians. People like my old pastor Ken, who in their humility have really shown forth the love and justice of God—personally, concretely. So, one of my ambitions is to be a great person like those saints one day. Have you known people like that in your life—people of exemplary service? Clearly not all Christians are this way, but some are. So, think about those folks--weren't they also people of remarkable humility? That's what I think of when I think of my old pastor, Ken—even when he was calling me out for my sense of entitlement, he was doing it out of love. Ken was humble, but he wasn't a doormat either.

Someday I want to be a saint like that—someone who can both serve and be served with grace. My grandparents were like that as well. I want to be like them someday—volunteering for meals-on-wheels, picking up litter while out on walks around the neighborhood. When I think of service, I think also of this former judge I met in Belfast who modeled hospitality for me in amazing ways. He had a smile and warm greeting for every person who walked by his office—no matter who they were. He didn't care if he'd see them ever again—he welcomed people just because they were fellow children of God. That's service. I remember getting that same kind of treatment from a custodian at an elementary school in West Seattle once too. Never have I seen anyone clean a building with such dignity—he said he did it because Jesus wants us to welcome little children and serve them. So, I want to be like him someday because there is joy in that kind of service.

There have been people in this community whose service has inspired me as well. I want to be like them someday. I want to join the communion of saints with Daisy Dawson and Thelma Ross. I love calling up Flossie Snipes on the phone these days—just hearing her voice makes me feel encouraged. I always look forward to seeing Ginny and Ernestine on Tuesdays because of the way they approach service in this place with such humility and grace. I don't mean to put you two on the spot, but it's true. And then there's Larry Low. It's hard to even get my head around all the ways that Larry serves people. I want to be like Larry—don't you?

I could go on like this, but you get the idea. God has given us one another to model this love and service of Jesus. As we continue to be loved and served through the grace of God, we all can grow into this powerful, countercultural sense of mutual service.

I'm reminded also of what Martin Luther King Jr had to say about his legacy, as he mentioned in his last sermon about how he'd like to be remembered, he said,

> "I'd like somebody to mention that day that Martin Luther King Jr. tried to give his life serving others. I'd like for somebody to say that day that Martin Luther King Jr. tried to love somebody.
>
> I want you to say that day that I tried to be right and to walk with them. I want you to be able to say that day that I did try to feed the hungry. I want you to be able to say that day that I did try in my life to clothe the naked. I want you to say on that day that I did try in my life to visit those who were in prison. And I want you to say that I tried to love and serve humanity.
>
> And that is all I want to say. If I can help somebody as I pass along, if I can cheer somebody with a word or a song, if I can show somebody he's traveling wrong, then my living will not be in vain."

May we go and do likewise, friends. As we have been served, let us serve one another, unto death and beyond. Amen?

Expect Nothing
Luke 19:28-40

There is a poem by Alice Walker that I remember reading in high school—it left quite an impression on me. It's called "expect nothing." It goes like this:

Expect nothing. Live frugally
On surprise.
become a stranger
To need of pity
Or, if compassion be freely
Given out
Take only enough
Stop short of urge to plead
Then purge away the need.

Wish for nothing larger
Than your own small heart
Or greater than a star;
Tame wild disappointment
With caress unmoved and cold
Make of it a parka
For your soul.

Discover the reason why
So tiny human midget
Exists at all
So scared unwise
But expect nothing. Live frugally
On surprise.

"Expect Nothing" by Alice Walker. I remember when I first read it, I thought I had found some solid advice for life—live frugally on surprise. It seemed like such a beautifully simple solution to all the frustration and disappointment that comes from getting our hopes up. If we could simply expect nothing—living only in the present moment, then we wouldn't take blessings for granted, and we wouldn't be bitter about missed opportunities—all of life would be one beautiful surprise. Part of that idea still resonates with me. I notice how much of my life has been lost to worry over the future—longing for things that have never happened or may still never happen. If only I could lower my expectations to the point of not needing a future at all. To simply rejoice in the now, to celebrate what is.

Then every moment that comes next would be a beautiful gift. Doesn't that sound great?

It's kind of biblical too. Jesus taught his disciples not to worry, not to fear. And in terms of expectations, this story of Palm Sunday seems to be case in point. All those people in the crowd that day, with such great expectations for who Jesus was and what he was going to do for them. They thought he would deliver them from their Roman oppressors—that he would lead them in some kind of armed revolt and a military victory; that finally the kingdom of David would be restored, and Jesus would sit on the throne as the King of Israel; to rule over them with justice and righteousness, to deliver them from poverty and fear and humiliation.

Let's wave our branches in celebration of this wonderful dream!

They had been waiting for this moment for so long, their expectations of Jesus were so high that day. In Luke's version of the events, he comes riding into the capitol city on a colt—a young horse that would presumably grow into a mighty war horse. They shouted out in celebration— "at last! Glory to God—Praise Heaven—Ride on, King Jesus—Save us!" Oh, their expectations were so great! So, no wonder their disappointment was also so overwhelmingly great that week. As the people quickly realized that Jesus wasn't really going to do any of those things. He wasn't going to lead a military revolt. He wasn't going to overthrow the Romans. He wasn't going to restore the Davidic Monarchy or instantly liberate the people of Israel from their political and economic oppression. The crowds threw this grand procession for him on Sunday and by Thursday night all Jesus had managed to do was to get himself arrested. What good was the man going to do from jail? No wonder the people were so severely disappointed. Their expectations were way too high! No wonder they were so angry and seemed to turn on him so quickly. On Friday instead of praising God for Jesus, many were shouting "crucify him!"

This seems extreme to us now in retrospect, and we tend to be a bit embarrassed by it, but have you ever been disappointed this deeply by someone?

Have you ever had high expectations for someone—a friend, a family member, a lover, only to have that person trample all over your hopes and dreams? Have you ever had your heart ripped in two like that? I trust that most of you probably already have a person in mind by now. Hold on to that memory—though I know it's painful. Try to remember when that wound was fresh. What did you want to do to that person in your anger? What did you want to see happen to that person after he or she had betrayed you? Don't say it out loud—you can keep that one between you and God, just remember how you felt. The greater the expectations, the greater the loss, the greater the pain, the greater the wrath. Am I right?

So, an easy corrective to this cycle would be to dispense with the expectations! "Expect Nothing! Live frugally on surprise." Don't let yourself hope or love or long for something more, because you're just setting yourself up for disappointment. Take your fragile little heart and lock it away—protect it! Lest it be broken again. Because who needs that kind of pain?

Those of us who identify with the Reformed Tradition have a theological term for this—we call it the doctrine of absolute depravity. Which is a fancy way of saying we expect the worst from people all the time. That way we're never disappointed, just sometimes pleasantly surprised when it doesn't go that way. The key is to avoid giving too much power to people, you see, lest they misuse it. We don't put people in positions where they are likely to disappoint us. We don't put people on pedestals—no saints, no heroes. Taken to an extreme this might even mean avoiding relationships altogether, since any relationship involves expectations. People begin to say, "Let's not get married, because marriage doesn't work—we'd just be setting ourselves up for failure." Or "who needs mentors? Wasn't our parent's disappointment enough? Politics? Advocacy? Please. Voting is about choosing the lesser evil. Church membership? Not after the last bad experience. Those people can turn on you too." Do you all see what I'm getting at?

It begins with a simple, and a natural desire to avoid pain. We all do this. We lower our expectations of people to avoid being hurt by them. We close ourselves off from disappointment, we protect ourselves. We refuse to join in the crowd all together lest they disappoint us. But how easily those low expectations instead turn to cynicism and separation. How quickly we find ourselves all alone—not without pain, just pain of a different sort—the pain of loneliness

In the end it doesn't work—this "Expect nothing" business. It just makes things worse. So, what are we to do?

Well I'll tell you what Jesus did. This is the story of Palm Sunday, where he chooses to join in the crowd anyway. Jesus wasn't naïve. He knew what was going to happen to him in Jerusalem, how the crowds would react once they realized he wasn't going to meet their expectations. Jesus knew exactly how this drama was going to go down, and yet he went through with it anyway. He got involved anyway! Jesus went through with the whole shebang—the whole enchilada—the complete package--from the hosannas and pageantry on Sunday to the horror of the cross on Friday. Instead of turning away from the pain, he embraced it! Instead of lowering expectations, he helped fan the flame! Isn't that crazy?

Consider this: Jesus could have *walked* into the city of Jerusalem that day, as he had many times before. He could have gone incognito to avoid all the hoopla. He could have worn a mask while turning tables in the temple—maybe he could have even cyber hacked that institution. But instead Jesus went in fully on display. And he played it up. Sent a few guys ahead of the parade to get some royal transport. Told the disciples about a young horse he'd seen tied up on the way, "If anyone asks why you're taking the colt, tell them "The Lord" needs it." He said. "The *Lord* needs it" Yeah, that should do it. Can you imagine how word would travel about this King coming into town and commandeering vehicles? Jesus knew this would be the sign the people were looking for—an excuse to take to the streets, to wave branches and throw cloaks on the road. It was intentional—this street theater—like Jesus wanted the people to hope, to dream, to expect that something great was about to happen.

"Raise those palm branches again." Let's raise those expectations!

Now consider. If we were there today, knowing what we know now. Would we join in? Would we get caught up in the crowd and take part in the celebration, or would we hold back, hold up our hands and say, "wow—you know, I've seen where this ends up—I'm not sure I want to go there."

Friends, the good news of Palm Sunday is that Jesus goes there—he goes there--whether we are willing to or not. Jesus goes with, or without us. Jesus has enough hope and faith, even when we hide in the back and try to play it safe. He is willing to go into that place of trial, and pain, and disappointment because he knows there is life on the other side, and he wants to show us the way. You know the story—Jesus even comes back to tell us it was worth it. He comes back to say to us, "Come with me this time." Yes, it's risky, yes, people are fickle, yes you will likely get hurt at some point, but he also says, "I will be there with you, during the chaos and pain. And things will look even better once we've made it through together. So, come, celebrate with me know. Dare to risk, to hope, to dream. Come follow me into life in all its messiness. Expecting nothing doesn't fix anything. Cynicism doesn't 't make the world a better place. But faith, hope, love—these are things worth living for, even worth dying for.

I invite you to go back to that painful memory I directed you to a few minutes ago. You know that person or experience that you still avoid thinking about—the one that if possible, you would never like to revisit. If you feel comfortable doing so, go ahead and close your eyes as you reflect. If closing your eyes is also too risky, then keep your eyes open—we all can go into Holy Week with our eyes wide open. What would it be like to live that pain again this week? To celebrate today the joyful expectations that led you to your sense of loss. Imagine having that kind of hope again, that kind of unguarded joy. Imagine daring to hope for those kinds of experiences again! I invite you to praise God for all those memories, for how they make you who you are today—more resilient, wiser. And I invite you to ask God to give you the courage and boldness with which to move through that pain once again, in order that you too might find new life, and life to its full.

Please pray with me.

God of life and hope and unending joy. Thank you for experiencing the frailness of humanity through your son Jesus. Thank you for walking with us also through our pain and loss and disappointment. Thank you for promising to bring us also from death to resurrected life when we walk with you. Please help us this week, to know the joy of your unending love, and to go with your son Jesus also into places of darkness and pain so that we might experience something of your resurrection. We pray these things in his name. Amen.

The Seven Last Words
John 7

"Forgive Them, Father, for they know not what they do."

Forgive them, says Jesus, and as a white person I say, "Yes! Amen!" Forgive them. Forgive us! For our miserable sin of racism and white supremacy. Forgive us for the hundreds of years of slave trading and the lynching's and for Jim Crow and for Mass Incarceration. So many of us white folks are horrified when we learn the truth about the history of our country and how we as white people have not only benefited from but participated in the systematic subjugation of people of color. When we learn this, we feel so guilty, so ashamed, it comes as a great relief to hear this cry of Jesus' from the cross, because we too feel like we didn't know what we were doing, and all we want now is forgiveness. Forgiveness for our complicity, forgiveness for our ignorance, we want ongoing forgiveness for the implicit racial bias that we still carry--the stuff that we're still not aware of that we don't know what to do with. We white people often want and need this forgiveness that Jesus has.

And yet while many white Christians around the United States today are meditating on forgiveness, at the same time there are also a lot of people of color in the streets crying out rightly, not for forgiveness, but for justice. Have you noticed that? Because it's not enough just to forgive those who participate in state sponsored violence--we also need them to be held accountable for their actions so that it won't keep happening. We need justice too! You know I'm talking about all the police shootings of unarmed black men still going on today. This is another way we experience the crucifixion of Jesus.

Jesus says, "Forgive them Father, for they know not what they do." But does that let us off the hook? When black and brown people are unjustly pushed out of white neighborhoods and suspended from white-run schools and targeted by the police and sentenced and jailed at inordinate rates. Does Jesus simply give us white people a pass when we fail to speak up, when we fail to intervene?

People of color today cry out for justice, while White Christians say "Oh, but you have to forgive--Jesus says to forgive." So, let's take another quick look at forgiveness tonight. I'm a Presbyterian, which is a predominantly white denomination that values scripture and careful study, and we Presbyterians don't like to take verses like these out of context. So, I want to remember tonight a couple other things Jesus has to say about forgiveness. One of which is the Lord's Prayer. The prayer that Jesus taught us--you know how it goes, we're supposed to ask God to forgive us our sins, how? "As we forgive those who sin against us." This seems to imply that if we don't forgive others, then we will not be forgiven. Something for white people to think about there.

And then there was that other time Jesus said that if your neighbor has something against you, you should put aside your offering, go be reconciled with your neighbor, and then come present your gift in worship. So, there's got to be reconciliation with our neighbors before we can be reconciled with God. Also, interesting. Because people who study these things tell us that before you even get to reconciliation-- you've first got to have truth and reparations. Forgiveness requires an honest attempt to make it right!

So, to summarize, if we white people want to be forgiven, as Jesus clearly wants us to be forgiven, then we must 1. Forgive others. 2. Tell the truth about what we've done and 3. Give reparations--try to make it right. That's a bit more involved than a simple absolution, don't you think? It's a big ask but remember that with God all things are possible. And Jesus shows us the way. So, imagine it.

Imagine if we white people got serious about forgiveness, so that God would be more inclined to forgive us. Imagine, for instance, if we forgave not just white-collar criminals or disgraced politicians, but drug offenders and petty thieves, and all the relatively innocent black and brown people who spend time in our prisons. Can you imagine that kind of forgiveness? Or imagine us white people simply forgiving our POC neighbors when they get angry with us or make us feel guilty about our privilege. That's forgiveness too. And can you imagine forgiving our ancestors for putting us in this guilty situation to begin with? Can you imagine forgiving our parents and grandparents for teaching us so much prejudice and hatred? We white people have a lot of forgiveness to do in order to be forgiven.

And then there's the truth. Are we ready to be honest about our faults and our failings? Can we face the reality that every aspect of our society has been designed to lift white people up, while pushing down people of color? Can we even call it what it is--white supremacy? Say the words. White Supremacy. Can we tell the truth about the racism of our families and friends and institutions? Can we call out the truth about the guy white people elected to be President of the United States--that White Supremacy is what created Donald Trump and got him into power?

Even when we do all of that, that's only 2 out of 3 steps! There's still no reconciliation without reparations. We still won't be done making all things right.

So, what would it be like for white people to look at the Movement for Black Lives Platform, and to see the demand for reparations as a necessity rather than a wish? Can we understand as Christians that reversing the legacy of slavery is essential to our salvation--that we must put our money where our theology is in order to be forgiven and restored to right relationship in the kingdom of God. Can you imagine?

Friends, Jesus said he came into the world, not to condemn the world, but that it might be saved through him. And yet this is no cheap grace, it's no easy forgiveness. Jesus gave his very life in order to show us what it is we have been doing wrong--the injustice of it--and how we can make our way to forgiveness, difficult as that may be. May we go with him on the way to reconciliation, on this path of the cross, so that God's kingdom would come, and God's will would be done on earth as it is in heaven. Amen?

Beginning Again
Mark 16.1-8

Christ is Risen! Christ is Risen indeed! Hallelujah!

We have come to the end of the story, or at least the end of the gospel of Mark as it was first written. The stone is rolled back, and an angel announces that he is risen. Jesus of Nazareth, who was crucified. He has been raised. Praise be to God! Our celebration this morning is the culmination of the Lenten season of preparation. 40 days of fasting and praying and reflecting on this incredible story. During this season I have been doing a sermon series on the questions of Jesus--questions he asks us in this story like, "what is your name? Who do you say that I am? Why are you so afraid? Do you want to be well?" There was a large group of us that met here each Sunday night to walk together towards the cross and talk about these things--all that God has done and continues to do among us. So, I know I'm supposed to be happy that this season has reached its great conclusion at Easter. But we've been having such a good time together that I'm not quite sure that I am happy about it.

It's like when you've come to the end of a really great book or TV series. You know that feeling you have when you're super excited for the grand finale, but at the same time you don't want it to end? You wish it could keep going. You say to yourself, "Why did Heisenberg have to die?" And why does Downton Abbey have such a short season? It's crazy, isn't it?

Scripture is much the same way, you know. No, seriously. THIS is the greatest story ever told. And when the writer of the first Gospel, the gospel of Mark, when he or she finished this masterpiece about the life of Jesus-- complete with intrigue and betrayal and surprise reversals, it was clear that the story wasn't over--it could never be over, because Love never ends! That's why the narrative is left open-ended. The original last verse of the Gospel of Mark is incomplete--it reads, "so they went out and fled from the tomb, for terror and amazement had seized them, and they said nothing to anyone they were afraid, for . . ."

Yes, it ends in a preposition. English teachers would hate this, but fortunately it was written in Greek, and our translations have covered up the grammar. For centuries people thought this ending was a mistake--they thought the author must have been confused or distracted or simple-minded. Some early scribes wrote their own endings to the gospel because they couldn't stand the way that finale left them hanging. There were so many loose ends--so many questions left unanswered! Like why is Jesus back in Galilee? And do the disciples follow the angel's instructions to meet him there? Will they live happily ever after? Inquiring minds want to know!

But we who have been looking at the questions of Jesus this season should know by now that this is totally consistent with the way Jesus himself would have wanted the story written. Jesus asked a lot of questions in his three short years of ministry--about 40x more questions than he answered, depending on how you count them. So why shouldn't this story end with more questions than answers? Even the last words of Jesus in Mark's gospel are in the form of a question. In the Gospel of John, he says "It is finished." But here we are left with Jesus crying from the cross: "My God, My God, why have you forsaken me?" That question just hangs there for us to think about, even after the resurrection. "Why have you forsaken me?"

No wonder the women who came for his body were afraid, terrified at the news that he had been risen. The man in white says to them, "'Jesus isn't here. Go, tell his disciples and Peter that he is going ahead of you to Galilee; there you will see him, just as he told you." But these disciples aren't so sure if they want to try again. They aren't sure if they will go meet Jesus in Galilee--the place where it all began. After-all look where the journey took Jesus last time--to rejection, betrayal, to an agonizing death on the cross. The disciples aren't sure if they really believe that he is back, that Jesus is risen, and even if he is--what then?

So, in reading this grand conclusion to the story we are left with this ultimate question of Jesus, this time left for a messenger to deliver. Will we flee? Or will we follow? Knowing now for certain that when Jesus calls us, he calls us to come and die.

This morning we will be welcoming 12 disciples into membership with this congregation--people who have faced this question, wrestled with the whole story, and still said, "Yes, we want to keep going. We want to go back to the beginning and read it all over again. We want to keep trying to make sense of these questions, together, in community, trusting that as we do so Jesus will be with us. We will trust that God is with us in this messy drama we call faith. We know it won't be a perfect story going forward." These 12 surely aren't any more gifted or faithful than those first 12 fishermen who walked with Jesus. But it is a hopeful sign, isn't it? That the story isn't over? That God is still at work in this place? Indeed, when you read the book of Acts, you start to see that this is far from the end of the line in terms of what God wants to do with us. Maybe the best is yet to come! Because now when we re-read this story, we do so with the wisdom of those who have been there before.

We get to re-enact this drama of faith as those who have already faced some demons and seen some healings and let Jesus wash our feet.

Do you ever wish God would give you a do-over? Have you wondered what it would be like to go back to some part of your life and try it over again, knowing what you know now? What if that's part of what resurrection means for us? God declaring to us that it's not over. Our stories aren't over. No matter how long it's been since we were in the thick of it. Still we get to go back and try again. This time with the assurance that God's got our back. So, this time we can let go of some power and control. This time we can make some different choices. We can ask for help. We can change our role in the drama from one of domination to one of service. We can stand up to the powers of oppression and violence still at work in the world. We can do our part to overcome structures of racism and patriarchy. We can work to undo the exploitation of the poor. The exploitation of the earth. The story isn't over, friends--it continues! Even beyond the point of death!

And for some of us it is literally just the beginning--this story. In a little bit we'll also have the joy of baptizing three babies that have been born to members of this congregation. Children of the promise that God will continue the story in them! It can be a little scary, the idea of giving over our precious little ones to the costly way of Jesus. The white clothes traditionally used in baptism are meant to remind us again of this part of the story--of a young man dressed in a white robe sitting next to the empty tomb. It is the costume of a martyr--one who has been crucified with Christ--what a frightening sign to put on a baby. But it is also a sign of victory and assurance, because it symbolizes the whole journey--returning to the beginning with Jesus' baptism in the river Jordan, when the Spirit of the Lord descended on him like a white dove, and a voice from heaven declared, this is my son, the Beloved, with whom I am well pleased. It's a reminder of the transfiguration, when Jesus was lit up like a night light, assuring the disciples that God was with them during their ministry. And then in the end it reminds us that that even after God's beloved children have faced trouble in the world--rejection, betrayal, maybe even crucifixion--God promises to never leave them or forsake them, to overcome death itself on their behalf, and to roll away the stone so that they too can begin again.

If only we could all remember this on a daily basis--this sign and seal of God's grace toward us. If we remembered the whole story, wouldn't we perhaps be filled with less fear? Perhaps a little more willing to go back to the beginning and try following Jesus again?

Hear the good news of the gospel, friends: Jesus is risen--the heavy lifting has already been done! The stone is rolled away, and the story continues back in Galilee, where Jesus goes before us, making a way for us to begin again. Because God's love for us never ends. Will we go to meet him? Will we also commit to joining him along the way in this story of tragedy and triumph and everlasting life?

Paul and Silas in Prison
Acts 16:16-34

Hey, it's great to be back with you all today after a week away with my family in Southern California. I'm glad that while I was gone Bianca felt called to preach last Sunday on the mission statement of Jesus in Luke 4, since it's also the mission of the church that underlies today's reading from the narrative lectionary—the story of Paul and Silas' adventure in prison.

Jesus said in his first public sermon, "The spirit of the Lord is upon me, God has anointed me, to preach good news to the poor. God has sent me to proclaim freedom to the prisoners and recovery of sight to the blind, to set the oppressed free." Luke 4:18. Then later, before his death and resurrection and ascension into heaven, Jesus told his disciples, "Whoever believes in me will do the things I've been doing, and even greater things." John 14:12-14

So that's what we see happening in the early church here in the book of Acts. This is the third time in the book we read about people getting broken out of prison, because that's what God does. And that's what the Holy Spirit intends to continue to do through us—to set the prisoners free.

It's a particularly relevant mission given the situation of mass incarceration in this country. If we are serious about our mission of seeking the Beloved Community through this *LIBERATING* love of Jesus, then we have some specific work to do. The work of getting people out of jail. I believe Jesus meant this literally.

So, I'm grateful for the opportunities I have personally to participate in this work of liberation. On Friday, thanks to Rick Derksen's leadership, I got to take part in an action of the No New Youth Jail campaign--the people's moratorium in which about 10 people got arrested, including a few clergy persons. And I find this to be encouraging work. There now is a large coalition of people working against the construction of a new youth jail in this part of the city. There are more and more people who recognize that locking people up, and youth in particular, is not good for them or for our society. People are admitting that prisons don't do rehabilitation, they're an act of retribution. So, if our county is going to spend $210 million dollars on juvenile justice, the people most affected are saying that it should be directed toward restorative justice programs, not on the prison industrial complex. And we certainly don't need a new facility with two or three times the current capacity. We need to build schools and housing, not prisons. We should be setting kids free, not locking them up! This isn't just a liberal agenda, it's the mission of God. Amen?

But I know that for many people it's not quite that simple. I know that not everyone is with me in saying Amen to this campaign. I'm also friends with people who work on the inside of the current youth jail, and they understandably see things differently. Some of you may be aware that we have one of our church members, Jared, who has been doing chaplaincy work at the jail through his studies at Seattle University, and he has felt God's spirit powerfully at work within the structure of that institution. I haven't talked with him about the anti-jail movement very much, but I have talked to another friend--a guy named Jon-- who oversees a chaplaincy program there, and he also told me once that he has mixed feelings about the whole thing. While my chaplain friend, Jon, sympathizes with the protestors, at the same time he told me about kids he works with who he believes really need the jail. They aren't ready to be released yet. Jon said "Some of these youth are grateful for the time they have in lock-down, because it gives them the space, they need to make some changes in their lives. Some kids need the jail." That's what Jon said to me. And my friend also went on to explain how he worries what would happen if there really was no youth jail, because he expects that some kids would then simply be sent to an adult facility—which would be much, much worse. And I had to agree that this makes a certain amount of sense--to have a youth jail as an alternative to the adult jail. It's hard to even imagine a world in which jails don't exist. So, I can also support those who try to work within the existing structure. I understand this argument some politicians have for wanting to spend $210 million to make the youth jail more hospitable—a nicer place to be locked up. They believe a youth jail is necessary, and the current one is decrepit. I get that.

What I have a problem with is that they are expanding the facility. The need for space has been going down, but they are making it bigger--two or three times the needed capacity. $210 million dollars. To put this in perspective, there are only about 20-40 kids in residence there on any given night, so that works out to about 5.5 million *per room* or $750 per child, per night for next 20 years.

This seems like a ridiculously bad deal to me, which is one reason I lend my support to the No New Youth Jail movement. But again, I get why people on the inside of the jail might have a hard time imagining an alternative. Because, after-all, their paychecks also depend on the existence of the jail. There are a lot of people whose jobs exist because of that $210m budget. They are in a sense, profiting off the system of incarceration. We wouldn't call them jailers—exactly--nobody wants that kind of label, and chaplains are far from jailers, but they are part of the system. Just like we are. We ordinary citizens are also part of this system of mass incarceration whether we like it or not, because we pay taxes whether we like it or not, and our taxes are going to build this jail. So, we too are paying to lock up kids. And we also benefit from not having troubled youth loose in our society. Many people see this as a reasonable arrangement.

With that in mind I invite you to take another look at this story from the book of Acts. Let's consider again what setting people free looks like in this example from scripture.

The way the story goes is that Paul and his buddy Silas are going about their business of preaching and teaching in public when they come upon a woman who has an unfortunate gift of prophecy. They don't find her, she finds them. This random woman starts following Paul and Silas around, shouting "Those guys are servants of the highest God." It's true what she's saying, but she's advertising it in a distracting way. It probably felt like this oppressed woman was obnoxiously stealing Paul and Silas' thunder and interrupting their sermons, pointing at them and saying, "They're telling you the way to be saved!" It's disruptive, it's embarrassing. And she keeps at it until Paul and Silas are deeply annoyed and fed up. She's like that woman in Jesus' parable who keeps bothering the judge until he gives her justice, just so that she'll leave him alone. Paul and Silas don't want to be pulled into this woman's drama, they don't want to get involved at all, but she's disturbing their peace. Her prophetic gift is disturbing the peace! And that's when they decide to do something about her situation.

This I think is noteworthy. So often we think of Paul and Silas as being the liberators here, but it seems like this woman is also freeing these men from their complacency. Do you see that? She's the one answering Jesus' call to give people sight, to cure them of their moral blindness. And she does it by disturbing the peace. It's interesting.

Anyway, it turns out Paul and Silas don't even have to do much to help her. All it takes is a few words in the name of Jesus and this woman is set free. Suddenly, she realizes she doesn't have to tell fortunes anymore. She doesn't have to turn tricks. She doesn't need those two men who were making money off her gifts, either. She can simply walk away from her captivity. So, she does. And that's the last we hear about her. Another unnamed woman who exemplifies faith.

But now Paul and Silas, whose eyes have now been opened to an exploitative relationship, these two guys who have casually used their privilege to intervene, now THEY are accused of being disturbers of the peace. So, they take her place as the focus of the drama. That's noteworthy too. When people use their voices to speak up about injustice, they often then become targets of the system. You see how that works? This is what happened to Jesus too. Paul and Silas become scapegoats, just like Jesus was. When disciples take on Jesus' mission, they also take on his suffering.

So, the pimps/corporate lawyers of the story take Paul and Silas to court for disrupting their business model. The woman's liberation was an economic problem for them--they were out of a job! Never mind that they had been profiting off this woman's oppression. They say that Paul and Silas had no right to set the woman free. The former slave-owners trump up charges against the two disciples, just like they did to Jesus, and the crowd starts to chant, "Lock them up, lock them up!" Does it sound familiar?

Well I think next scene has some resonance too. Paul and Silas surely already know what is going to happen next, because it has happened before. The disciples are chained to the floor of a prison cell, singing songs of praise to God in the middle of the night. "We who believe in justice shall not rest! We who believe in justice shall not rest until it comes!" They sing with confidence because they know that our God is a God of freedom, a God of liberation. Paul and Silas may have been reluctant to see that woman's oppression to begin with, but now they are the ones calling out to God for release, and they know that God will answer. And sure enough. There's a crash and a bang. The ground starts shaking like it did when Jesus died. Their chains break free, like they did when Jesus descended to hell. The doors to the prison break open, like the stone being rolled away from the tomb. "Free at last, Free at last. Thank God almighty," they say!

But there's a problem. And this is the best part. Maybe the most significant part of the story. The problem is that if Paul and Silas just get up and leave, then the jailer will get in trouble for having let them go free. The disciples would be letting someone else take their place—someone else would have to pay the price for their freedom. And that wouldn't solve anything. The system would continue. That's how the retribution system works, you see. Paul and Silas free the slave woman, so they must take her place. If Paul and Silas go free, the prison guard will have to take their place. But Jesus came to interrupt that cycle. The disciples also want to interrupt it. So, in following Jesus, Paul and Silas decide to stay. They decide *not* to walk away, *not* to use their freedom to be indifferent or uninvolved. Just like Jesus up on the cross. People called out to him, saying "If you're the son of God, free yourself!" But Jesus chose to stay there in that place of danger, calling out to his oppressors, "Forgive them Father, for they know not what they do." And that's what Paul and

Silas do as well. They stay there, in a broken prison—a system that they helped break. They stick around to use the freedom they've been given in Christ to proclaim freedom even to their jailor. To preach forgiveness to him. To cure his blindness, just as God has cured theirs. And that's what really disrupts the system. People don't know what to do with that kind of liberation—the kind that frees not only the oppressed, but the oppressors.

It's interesting how at the end of the story we still don't hear what happened to the liberated woman. Or the other prisoners who were freed along with Paul and Silas. It's the jailer who becomes the center of the story. He and his whole family are saved. They too are set free. He doesn't have a job anymore--the prison is gone, but the jailer comes away with his life. And this time it's a life that doesn't depend on locking up other people. That's what Jesus does for people--he gives us new life, a better life, life to its full.

Back to the No New Youth Jail movement. I don't expect you all to agree with me about the politics of that campaign. I simply want to point out this morning that God clearly cares about liberation, but not just the liberation of others, also the liberation of ourselves. We who also participate in systems of oppression. God wants to set us free. And I invite you to reflect on how it happens in this story.

Think about how Paul and Silas are given new eyes to see--because of an oppressed woman who annoys them. Because of someone who is disturbing the peace. Does God ever put people like that in our way? Could God be trying to use those people to free us somehow?

And then when Paul and Silas do get involved. Notice how they use their experience as an opportunity to liberate others. Not just the people in jail, but the jailer too. Paul and Silas act as if the jail itself isn't even what matters--they're there to free the jailer as well as the prisoners, they care just as much about the guy in charge. So, who does God want us to liberate? Are there powerful people in our lives who also need to be set free? How can we show up for them? The jails may still need to go away, but how can we reach out and assure the jailers that we still care about them, too?

Friends, I know it's a messy, complicated world we live in, and politics are hard to navigate. But hear the good news that God is at work to set us free. God will continue putting people and opportunities in front of us in order to liberate *us*. From complacency. From confusion. From oppression and from complicity. Paul once wrote that we must work out our salvation with fear and trembling. But take heart--often all we must do is stand firm together, sing a few songs of faith, and it is the system that trembles, it is the system that falls apart, and it is the freed people of God who are left shouting, "do not be afraid! We are still here! And We shall not be moved!" Amen?

Spiritual Jujitsu
Philippians 4:1-9

Today is the last Sunday that the lectionary has us in the short book of Philippians, and it's only here in Chapter 4, toward the end of the letter that Paul gets around to addressing what may have been one of the main reasons for writing to the church in Philippi--some ill feelings between a couple leaders of the congregation. We aren't told much about these two women Euodia and Syntyche, except that for some reason they were not of the same mind, even though they had both struggled alongside Paul in the work of the gospel, together with Clement and the rest of his co-workers.

Do you ever have to work with people who are not of the same mind as you? People who may have a different perspective on what you are doing, people who sometimes disagree with you, people who may at times seem like they are out of their minds? If you already have some-ONE in mind, then congratulations, you are human. Sometimes even people we love the most--our family members or our brothers and sisters in the church, even in Christian community we can have sharp disagreements. Disagreements that provoke arguments or passive-aggressive behavior that leads to feelings of hurt, anger, or distrust. And sometimes you can get these reactions even without some initial conflict. Have you ever met someone and realized right away that you just don't like him? Or her. Maybe no reason that you can name (or that you want to name), you just can't stand that person.

This simply happens from time to time, and the worst part about this feeling for Christians, is that we know these are the very people we have been called to love. These people who are sometimes of a different mind. We remember that God became reconciled to us in Christ Jesus in order that we might be reconciled with one another--especially within the household of faith. "Love your neighbors" Jesus said to us--"even your enemies." "Love one another as I have loved you" Painfully, sacrificially, even when you disagree.

So that's what we try to do, right? When we see that person who we have a hard time getting along with, we put on a brave face and try to be as kind as we can possibly be. We muster all our strength to forbear that person, taking deep breaths, checking our assumptions, using "I" statements--recalling of all those non-violent communication skills that make for better working relationships.

Syntyche: "So what I hear you saying, Euodia, is that you totally disagree with me and think my perspective is without value. Is that right?"

Euodia: "No, what I said was that that was the stupidest thing I've ever heard, and I wish you would just admit that you don't know what you're talking about."

Syntyche: "Oh! Well, thank you for your honesty. I really appreciate your being willing to talk this through. I wonder if there is some alternative that might be acceptable to both of us. . ."

Euodia: "I doubt it."

Syntyche: ---Serenity now--Serenity now--1001, 1002. . .

This is part of what Paul is calling the church to in this section of Philippians. To forbear one another--be patient, forgiving. "Let your gentleness be known to all" he says. Gentle being a loose translation for a word meaning something more like "generosity toward others." I love that advice--be generous toward others. Those cantankerous, difficult people--give them some slack, you never know what their back-story really is or what is going on for them in the moment.

And Paul gives a great piece of coping advice too. The way a therapist might say it today would be that we can focus on the positive. "Be positive." "Go to your happy place." Paul says, "Whatever is true, whatever is honorable, whatever is just, whatever is pure, whatever is pleasing, whatever is commendable, if there is any excellence and if there is anything worthy of praise, think about these things." Focus on the positive!

Euodia: "You are a selfish, miserable person, Syntyche. This team would be so much better off without your inane opinions."

Syntyche: "What's that? Oh, sorry--I was listening to my positive music station. Isn't it a beautiful day out there? I read online this morning about a dog that saved a blind man from a burning building. Isn't that awesome? Oh, and I love that color on you--seriously, that shirt looks great with your eyes."

This isn't a bad strategy, is it? I've met some curmudgeonly Christians who would do well to focus on this bit of worldly wisdom, because it IS such good advice. But notice that this idea is buried within Paul's larger point, because what really makes a difference in our relationships over the long-term isn't just learning better communication skills or figuring out how to regulate our own emotions. If you've tried to forebear others on your own strength, then you already know that you can only keep it up for so long before you crack, before you lose it with this person that rubs you the wrong way.

No, Paul's prescription for addressing conflict is much more sophisticated than simply "be patient." Or "remember to breathe." What Paul asks of the community here is something much better. I've heard it described as spiritual jujitsu. Which I hope makes sense even though I know nothing about martial arts.

The idea is to address one aspect of your life indirectly by working actively in some other area of your life. This is what spiritual disciplines are often all about. If you say to yourself. "I want to be more spiritual--I'm going to love God more." And what you do is you wake up each day telling yourself, "I'm going to love God, I am going to love God." This may help for a while, but eventually you may simply get tired and realize that you don't feel any different about God despite all that self-talk. Because loving God isn't so much about us, or our self-talk. That's just not how it works. Instead we must start doing the things God wants us to do to--serving others, showing up for community worship, giving to help those in need, being reconciled to our enemies. Then one day we might wake up and realize that we suddenly do love God more deeply, because our lives have been changed, and our hearts along with them.

That's how it is with reconciling relationships also. We can sometimes deal with them indirectly--by working on our own spiritual practices.

Two women in the church are having problems with one another. Paul doesn't say, "I want you to sit down with Syntyche and Euodia and work out a compromise." That may be partly helpful, but it's not going to solve the conflict long term, No, instead Paul says to them and to us, "Rejoice in the Lord always." Rejoice IN THE LORD. This is the pathway to better relationships, to sharing in the mind of Christ. Rejoice together, in the Lord. Let this be our focus and our goal. Sure, we may have our differences, our disagreements, but no matter what happens we can still have joy in Christ's reconciling presence among us. Christ who lived and died and was raised, for us, that our names might be written in the book of life. When this is our center, the joy of our hearts, then we already can give thanks in all circumstances. Then we really don't have to be anxious or worried about anything--including our conflicts, because we know that when we pray together, with thanksgiving, in the name of Jesus--whenever two or three of us agree on anything, including the healing of relationships, it will be done for us. So maybe instead of spending time bickering, we can refocus on making our requests known to God, and trust that the peace of God, the Shalom of God, which surpasses all understanding, will guard our hearts and minds in Christ Jesus. Love God first, and everything else follows. Get it?

The good news, friends, is that we don't have to face the difficult relationships of our lives alone, for the God of peace is with us. And when we focus our lives and our energy on Christ, this peace will be ours during those relationships.

I heard about a hostage crisis some years ago. A man boarded a school bus with a gun, threatening the driver and all the kids. The driver played a big part in ultimately talking the man down and the situation was resolved peacefully. Afterwards a reporter asked the driver how she was able to be so calm during the crisis, and she said to him "Well, I pray a lot." I pray a lot. Not "I prayed that the man wouldn't shoot me." Or "I prayed for serenity." She said "I pray a lot" --as in all the time. If you want to be cool under fire, make sure the God of peace is with you. With thanksgiving let your requests be known to God--frequently, and you will know God's shalom.

And we can help one another to find this peace--the peace that surpasses all understanding. Again, not just through breathing and communication, but by modeling compassionate consideration of others, and by urging one another to take on the mind of Christ--his mind of humility and service, and patience endurance.

There is a saint of the Catholic Church who illustrates this well for us. St Therese of Lisieux was a Carmelite nun who lived near the end of the 19th century in France. She is known for having developed a simple and practical approach to spirituality in her short life. Therese has come to be known as The Little Flower, because she lived a quiet life and saw herself simply giving glory to God as a little flower among the other flowers of Christ's garden. When Therese entered the convent at the age of 15, she quickly realized that she didn't seem to have the strength to live into the righteousness of her religious calling. The convent didn't ask anything heroic of her--she spent her days cooking and cleaning, painting, writing, and praying. But Therese felt incapable of the tiniest love, the smallest expression of concern and patience and understanding. So, she surrendered her life to Christ with the hope that he would act through her and help her over time to become more like Jesus. She took on the words of St. Paul, "I can do all things in him who strengthens me." And "all things" meant for her simply the daily grind of life.

Well in the nine years Therese served as a nun before dying of tuberculosis at age 24, she wrote a memoir in which she described a woman in her community who she had a hard time getting along with. This other woman must have had a difficult personality, and it sounds like she wasn't a particularly good nun, and Therese felt terribly afflicted with feelings of disgust and anger toward her. But instead of shunning this woman or confronting her, or trying to forget about her, Therese considered it part of her calling to love this woman as if she were Christ himself. Her memoir never named the woman, but Therese wrote at length about how difficult she was to live with--how often she just couldn't stand the site of this community member, yet how also being in her presence forced her to pray more fervently than ever, "Lord Jesus Christ, son of God, have mercy on me, help me to glorify you in my weakness." Therese wrote about how this conflict caused her to seek even more the mind of Christ, in order to love this neighbor as she loved herself. In order to press on to take hold of the prize for which she was called heavenward in Christ Jesus.

After her death, many years later when Therese would have been middle-aged, when her writings became well known and she was already being considered for canonization, this difficult companion of hers was interviewed by others and she remained oblivious as to Therese's true feelings. Instead she was known to say, "I don't know why it was that Therese loved me more than anyone else in our community, but she clearly did. She went everywhere with me and often sought me out for counsel. She told me often how much she gave thanks for me. And I'm glad I was able to be a blessing to her during her brief life."

Friends, Therese wasn't particularly special in her gifts or abilities--we are all saints of God. What made her great, was that she realized she didn't have the strength to love people on her own, and instead she rejoiced in God's strength--relying on prayer in order to maintain a generous attitude toward others. Just like other people, she got grumpy from time to time, but she didn't let other people make her anxious or upset. Instead she followed Jesus in giving thanks in all circumstances by focusing on whatever is honorable, just, pure, commendable--even just the beauty of little flowers.

And since our names also are written in the book of life, alongside that of St Therese, I urge you, as Paul urged us, to keep on doing these things that we have learned and received and heard and seen in our forbearers of faith--letting our graciousness toward others be known to all. That we too might know in full the presence of the God of peace, and that that Shalom might guard our hearts and minds together, in the one mind of Christ Jesus. Amen?

Why Church?
Hebrews 10

Today we have one final excerpt from the book of Hebrews for the year, and in this section the author seems to sum up the purpose of the book, which was to give a purpose for the community following Jesus' death and resurrection. So that's what I'm going to try and do for you all this morning. Those of you who have been around Madrona Grace for a while may have noticed that this is a recurring theme in my preaching, and you may even feel like I am preaching to the choir again this morning. But like the author of this sermon to the Hebrews, I believe it's important to review on a regular basis why it is that we're here. Don't you? Because it's easy to forget.

As we all get pulled in different directions by our work and family obligations we can start to wonder if church is worth the effort. We may sometimes wonder if maybe church is one of those things that used to be helpful but isn't so much anymore. Perhaps we feel we've outgrown it or evolved beyond it somehow. Of course, there is the whole evangelism problem too—how when you invite people to church these days, a lot of times the response is one of indifference, as in "Why would I want to do that?" And then we don't really know what to say next. And then there's also the challenge of fellow Christians who have given up on the church for various reasons. I meet Christians all the time who admit they don't go to church anymore because it doesn't meet their needs, or they just haven't found the right "fit." They've clearly bought into a mentality of consumerism when it comes to faith.

In response to these problems, some churches have been successful in keeping people and growing their congregations by embracing a culture of fear. As in "you better come to church, or God is going to be mad at you." Don't forget about the whole doctrine of H-e-double hockey sticks! That's one way to keep 'em coming back. Usually this goes along with some "beware of the evil of the world" theology too. As in--stick with us because we're the one truly righteous church--we can keep you safe from all the heathen out there and help you become perfect like we are.

Before I go on, let me assure you that these are NOT perspectives we support at Madrona Grace. And the reason for this is because these are not perspectives we believe are supported by scripture as a whole—and certainly not in this letter to the Hebrews.

It appears the community this letter was written to have some similar challenges when it came to identity and purpose, only in a Jewish context.

And the author had a very different response than one of inducing fear or guilt. Here's the situation Hebrews was written to address:

Before Jesus come, there was a sense that God was always on the brink of anger and wrath when it came to the people of God because they simply never measured up. The people could never be righteous enough or faithful enough, because only God is perfectly righteous and faithful. There were all these laws to help people get it right, but still God's people would fail, day after day, week after week. It was thought that this made God really, really angry, because God was like this authoritarian parent up in the sky, scowling down at the people, shaking a gnarled finger, saying "I told you not to make idols, I told you to keep the Sabbath holy—and now I'm going to have to strike you down, I'm going to have to punish you and teach you a lesson." And the only way to appease God's anger was to offer sacrifices for the sins of the people. There was a whole complicated system for doing this—with priests and animals and all these different regulations.

Incidentally some Christian churches today still have this image of a wrathful God, and sacrifices are still made to appease him—with tithes and offerings and church attendance and refraining from all sorts of worldly activities—usually things that are pleasurable. Did anyone here grow up with that kind of God? It's a system that seems to persist because it piggybacks on certain institutions like patriarchy and racism.

But the main point of Hebrews is to remind us that Jesus did away with all of that. He gave himself over as the sacrifice for sins—for all sins—for all time. So that no one should have to worry about sacrifices anymore. Not animal sacrifices, not other kinds of sacrifices. If God was ever angry to the point of wrath, we don't have to worry about that either because Jesus paid it all. Amen? Jesus, the perfect sacrifice, made it so that all God has left for us is love—unconditional, everlasting, abundant, all-encompassing love.

And one of the reasons we come to church each week is simply to be reminded of this. So that we can let go of all the internalized hatred and wrath that other people in our lives have heaped upon us. So that we can let go of some of the perfectionism and punitive tendencies that we sometimes still carry around with us and unleash on others. In a sense, this community can be a refuge from the world, because bad theology is still out there. It's in our families, it's in our places of work, it's in our neighborhoods, in our country, it's in our violent, vengeful world. And the church has resources to help with that.

But we're not the only ones who can help with it. That's one of the other things Jesus did that complicated things a little bit. Before Jesus, there was a sense that only Jewish people had access to the one holy, righteous, eternal creator of the universe. Everybody else was just worshipping idols. If non-Hebrews wanted in on the covenant between God and the chosen people, then they had to convert to Judaism and get circumcised. Again, some Christians still have vestiges of this theology today. They might not come out and say that you must be baptized to be saved, or that you must be in their church, but still they have a way of looking down on everybody else. Have you noticed that? And I hope you don't take what I'm saying this morning in the same vein, because I truly believe, and the Presbyterian Church (USA) states in writing that Jesus changed all of that. Jesus took a look at the old covenant with Israel, and said, good—that's fine, you can keep all of that if you like, but as the Son of God I'm also going to make a New Covenant, sealed in my blood, that says anyone who believes in my power to save will also have equal access to God. So, there is no one true church that's better than any other—we have all sinned and fallen short of God's glory, and we have all been redeemed by his sacrifice. Equally, all of us. Which means that I'm no better than you, or any other Christian. I may think I have better theology or that I'm more just than some other people, but I don't have a corner on the truth, and neither does our church! Unfortunately, that makes it hard to sell people on sitting through a 20-minute sermon, but this is the freedom we have been given—we don't actually *have* to be here.

And let me go even a step further. Because you know the other thing Jesus did? Besides getting rid of the whole wrath thing and letting everybody in on the covenant? He then poured out his spirit on all flesh. Jesus unleashed the Holy Spirit on the whole world. Not just Christians! All flesh. Meaning that God is already in the process of remaking our world, making all things new, stamping out injustice, comforting those who mourn, bringing forth the beloved community, and it doesn't even depend on us. We may be God's chosen people still—salt and light—God chooses to use us to bless others, but God can and does use other people too. Maybe even Muslims and Buddhists and Atheists. You never know how the Holy Spirit is going to move, it could be that She works despite the church sometimes, despite us. Isn't that crazy? There are so many amazing things going on in the world today around charity and peace-making and human rights. I'd like to be able to say that's all happening because of Christians—that that is why we are here—because we're leading the charge. But that would be misleading and simply untrue. We're not here because God needs us to bring about the Kingdom of God—the Holy Spirit does that, it doesn't all depend on us.

So, again, why are we here? That was the question this book of Hebrews was getting at. The people were saying to themselves, "So we don't have to make sacrifices anymore, and we don't even really have to follow the Jewish law anymore, so why are we meeting together again? It sounds like God has it handled."

Well from this letter I've got Seven reasons for you. Seven reasons why we're here—why it's worth it, why the Church still matters. See if there's one that resonates with you—one that maybe you could share with someone when it comes up that you go to church. 7 is a big number, I know, but I'll make it quick.

The first is that we're here to celebrate! We're here, friends to celebrate what God has done! To tell and retell the story of Jesus' victory over sin and death and fear, so that celebration permeates every part of our lives. And this can be fun, Amen? Church can and should be fun! We're here to sing and dance and rejoice in God's incredible love for us. Everybody loves a good party. So, let's do it up right! That's always my hope for worship, and I know we don't always get there, but it's the goal—to celebrate.

The second reason we are here is one I've already mentioned—call it liberation. We're here for liberation. Meaning we know that Jesus paid it all, that we have been set free, that the powers of sin and death have been overcome, but not everyone has gotten this message yet. There are still people who need to hear and live into this message, and we get to be an outpost proclaiming the good news of liberation and living it for all the world to see. We do this through inclusion, through hospitality, through building people up, week after week. This too is a good purpose for the church.

A third reason we are here is what happens after you've been liberated. Hebrews calls it assurance. We're here for assurance. Because we need to be assured again and again and again that it's not as bad as it appears. Especially like when things go down the way they did on Friday. We need to be reminded and to remind one another that God still loves us. God is still in control. No matter how many earthquakes there are in Haiti or terrorist attacks in Paris, or tragedies in our personal life stories—we need to be re-assured that God is not punishing us. We need to hear the good news that God is for us, not against us. That God laments and mourns with us in times of sorrow. That God's love for us never grows weary or cold. Hebrews says that because of Jesus, we can approach the throne of grace with a clear conscience, trusting that God will meet our every need.

So, comes number 4. We are here for hope! We're here for hope. Knowing that God loves us, and that God is faithful, Hebrews says let us be people of hope! Reminding one another that God is going to work it out. And this is deeper than simply being optimistic. South African Archbishop Desmond Tutu said once when asked about prospects for peace in the middle East—he said, he's hopeful but not necessarily optimistic. Optimism requires clear signs that things are changing, but our faith allows us to hope even when there are no signs of progress, because we place our trust in things yet unseen. Hope persists in the face of evidence to the contrary, undeterred by setbacks and disappointment. It's what keeps us going even in the worst of circumstance. So that's what we're here to do—to become people of hope, who don't get weighed down by all the bad news that comes our way, so we don't become cynical or bitter.

Reason number 5 to stick with the church. Vs 24 says we are here to provoke one another to love and good deeds. We are a provocative community. Do you ever feel like you need a reminder to give, to serve, to be a friend to someone in need? I know a lot of people these days don't feel like they need God to be or do good—and that's their business. But let me be the first to admit that I do need to be provoked occasionally. I believe truly I am a better person because of this community. Because you all provoke me to do better. It's not coercive or manipulative provocation, you all are simply a good influence on me. And this is part of what the church is for. How about you—do you need this kind of accountability in your life? Can you imagine admitting to someone out loud that you "need" to go to church?

The sixth reason we are here is for community. It's one of those things that's hard to define, but you know it when you have it. Do you feel like you have people to lean on in times of need? People to confide in, people to share your life with? How does that sense of community happen? One way to develop community is simply to spend time with others. That's why Hebrews encourages us to not give up meeting together. If you want real community, real friendship, then it takes time and commitment--once a month isn't going to cut it. Once a week will certainly help. But you know Churches don't work very well as community if you only see people on Sunday. We're not just here for worship, we're here for small groups, and service teams, and retreats and pilgrimages. We're here to share with one another and grow with one another in supportive community.

Which leads me to the 7th and final reason for Church from this book. We are here for encouragement. We need encouragement to live this life of faith to which we have been called. To help one another to show up and have hope. We're here to tell one another in a thousand different ways, that you can do it. Don't give up. Keep coming back. Jesus is with you and so are we, so hang in there! I imagine how hard life must be for people who don't get these kinds of messages on a regular basis. This is something that fuels my prayers for other people, imagining how lonely and discouraging it can be to try and get by without the encouragement of a healthy Christian community. I know plenty of people who say they are doing just fine, thank you very much, but how many others are lonely and hurting and trying to get by all by themselves?

Friends remember the word from Hebrews this morning. We're better off with celebration, and liberation, and assurance, and hope and provocation, and community, and encouragement. A pastor I once knew used to say that a Christian out of church is like a fish out of water—you don't last long. God may not need us to come to church, but we need these things in our lives. And we can rejoice that God has made them freely available—because God loves us. It is a gift to be able to say we get to go to church—thank God! Thank God that Christ died for us and rose for us, and lives now as our high priest, so that we can be here, now, in this place, celebrating together, loving one another, Seeking God's Beloved Community through the liberating love of Jesus. Amen?

The Beast
Revelation 13

It's great to be back with you today for another installment in this series on the Book of Revelation—this famously enigmatic grand finale to the Christian scriptures. If you missed a previous week like I did last Sunday, there are some notes in the back of the bulletin to help catch you up, but I'm not going to go over them again today because it's becoming too long of a list. Here it is on the screen. There's a lot to know about Revelation because it sums up the whole bible!

But thankfully today's message is relatively simple. Despite all the crazy symbolism involved, this epic battle in the middle chapters of the book really come down to how God deals with the beasts in our lives. So, I want to talk a little bit about beasts this morning.

Do you all know some beasts? Do you have beasts in your lives? It's not a word we use so much in everyday conversation—a bit antiquated maybe-very British sounding--like John Oliver saying— "he's such a beast!" For me the word recalls animals from the Harry Potter stories like griffins and dementors and giant snakes. I don't know if dementors would qualify as beasts since they're not very animal-like—they're ghostlier really, but I think it's interesting the way in that story they suck the joy out of people—that's very beastly or monstrous, which is the word we Americans would probably use. So, what are the beasts, or monsters at work in your life—the ones that attempt to suck the joy out of you—the demented things that try to take away your life?

For John of Patmos the monsters were mostly political in nature. A lot of the imagery in his vision is reminiscent of the Roman empire—there's a lot of speculation that one of the beasts in this chapter was meant to represent a specific emperor—Nero—one of the Caesars who persecuted the Jews and early Christians so famously in the first century. Because of this you could say that this 13th chapter of Revelation is sort of a counterpoint to the 13th chapter of Romans. Paul once wrote to his friends in Rome, telling them to obey the secular authorities because whatever authority they had was given by God. But then later, this pastor John writes to his friends elsewhere in the Roman empire, suggesting that this government had grown into a monster at war with God! It's quite the contrast. Some people see government as a helpful force for good, others see it as an oppressor. The same with the police depending on where you stand, right?

But how about you, would you count the American Empire as one of the beasts at work in your life? Do you see it as a monster or a power that has been authorized by God? And what other forces are at work in your life? I'm not talking about literal monsters—things with seven heads or 13 eyes and all that. You understand that we're talking in metaphor here. Another helpful comparison for this part of Revelation is that it's sort of like a political cartoon—you know one of those ones where the Republicans are portrayed as elephants and the Democrats are donkeys? John's animals are way creepier than that, but you get the idea. If you were to draw a cartoon of your life, what would the oppressors look like? Would they wear lots of watches, because they are always telling you to hurry up, hurry up—you're going to be late! Would they be super fat and have multiple mouths because they're always eating away at your self-esteem, trying to suck you dry?

I read a lot of children's books these days, because I have small children. I noticed that ever since Monsters Inc. came out there has been a proliferation of books about monsters. Have you seen some of these? The Little Shop of Monsters. Monster ABCs. The Monster Who Lost His Mean. They are very creative. I like how each monster seems to symbolize some small fear that children have. One monster is slick and slimy, another is sharp and poky. The tickle monster is particularly deceiving. Are you laughing or crying? Hohahahaha!

The real beasts in our lives are a lot harder to picture—which is probably why John's beasts are so bizarre. How do you make a caricature of loneliness? What kind of monster simply tries to make you look small? There are beasts in our world that have the ability to make us eat too much and drink too much and isolate ourselves and say mean things to the people we love. When we really sit down and take a look at the things in our lives that we're not proud of, usually there's some beast involved. We have names for many of them—Racism. Patriarchy. Unrestrained Capitalism. Militarism. This is just a few of the bigger ones—really it could be anything that plays on our fears and insecurities. Anything that keeps us heading in the wrong direction. Some of them might seem like good things on the surface—wealth, success, beauty. But when they distract us from what we know to be good and right and just—they become idols, they grow into monsters, no better than these ugly beasts of Revelation.

In the stories most of us grew up with there is a clear and simple plan for dealing with the beasts that oppress us. You fight them. Right? You slay the dragon. You hunt down the evil alien creature lurking in the depths of the sea, and you destroy it. This is the plot of most hero stories still today. Sometimes it's one superhero who takes care of the menace, other times a group of people band together to face down the threat. But there's a problem—what happens when the monster is too big to take down? What do you do when you feel powerless in the face of its destruction—when you've been dealing with it your whole life and still haven't overcome it? This is how John's churches felt in the face of the Roman empire. The way many people of color feel in the face of white supremacy. The way individual voters and wage laborers may feel in the face of corporate wealth.

More than a few Christians have gotten upset about the power of the beasts in this section of Revelation because they seem SO powerful—some people have seen this scripture as a magnification of their own fears about the end of the world, as if some great doom is scheduled to come down on us before Jesus returns. But this vision really says the opposite if you actually read it. The simple message of Revelation is that there's some nasty stuff at work in the world—monstrous stuff, yes, but relax—the Lamb of God is on it! Incidentally, here's another fun fact to share with Left Behind fans:

The word "Antichrist" does not appear in the book of Revelation. In 1 & 2 John an "anti-christ" is simply someone who denies that Jesus was the Christ—there were/are lots of them.

And these beasts also are dealt with every time we affirm that yes, Jesus is the holy one of God, who was and is and is to come. His is the power and the glory—the way toward life, and life to its full. The way of Jesus—his sacrifice, his humility, his love unto death—this is what saves us from the beasts, and indeed he has already saved us!

So again, here's how our story goes—the story of scripture—the story of God's people lived over thousands of years, and still active today, summed up in the book of Revelation. It's a bit surprising I think, that when faced with epic beasts of destruction, God's people aren't called upon to fight. Jesus even told us explicitly "do not violently resist an evil-doer." In John's vision some of his other words are also repeated—those who live by the sword die by the sword. Which is to say that it's not our job to slay the beast. Instead, we are simply called to stand in the face of it—to stare it down if you will, the way Max stares down the Beasts in Where the Wild Things Are— "Here is a call for endurance, and the faith of the saints" says John of Patmos. Because we believe that God in Christ has already overcome every power of sin and death—the battle has already been fought--and all we must do is wait for all things to be laid at God's feet. We don't fight, but we endure. We wait, we witness.

It's not very exciting or heroic, is it? It's certainly not the kind of thing that earns us honor or glory—simply enduring. But sometimes this is all we can do during suffering, is to endure. And in God's kingdom it turns out that this is enough! As we wait and endure and avoid going along with the monstrous forces at work in our world, we come to see how God is at work making all things new. When we let go and trust that God is in control—we find that those monsters and beasts, they get smaller and smaller. Their control and influence become less and less, until eventually they are no trouble at all. Because God had them shackled the whole time!

I once spent a year living in Belfast, Northern Ireland, working at a church and a community center during the whole Catholic/Protestant conflict they've been having over there for the last 400 years—what they call the Troubles. I tried to understand the politics of it, but never completely did—it just seemed like a total mess. The Catholics and the Protestants were like opposing political parties with some paramilitary forces thrown in. Sometimes one party would be winning, then the other party, and always there was violence—atrocities on both sides. "Sectarianism" as they call it there, is a beast. Well one day I asked the pastor of the church I was working at, a woman named Lesley, what she thought of the upcoming election, how the results would affect her. And she said to me simply, "You know, Mark, I can minister under any government." That's all she said--Mark, I can minister under any government. And I thought that was significant. It wasn't like Lesley didn't care who won. This pastor was certainly politically engaged. She wasn't saying the results didn't matter, but the fact is that she, and her community, and her work would endure no matter what power was in charge, because she believed that ultimately God is still in control, and none of these lesser powers will triumph in the end—this is our faith and witness.

Today, some 14 or so years later I'm happy to see that Northern Ireland has come a long way toward resolving their conflict—peace and reconciliation are indeed overcoming the powers of violence and hatred in that country, in large part because of people like Lesley who have continued to live and work trusting that God would see them through. Thank God for people who refuse to give in to fear or hatred, for those who come face to face with the fears that we all have—no matter what causes them and continue living as people of faith instead.

I invite you to come back to your personal beasts again for a minute. Your little antichrists. The ones that continue to give you grief from time to time—be they addictions, obsessions, the power of a corporation or an "ism" or an unfulfilled dream. Take a moment to close your eyes and picture your fear—maybe a fear of feeling poor, destitute, alone—maybe a fear of depression or memory loss or the loss of a friend. Imagine yourself holding these beasts and fears up to the light. Asking what is the worst these things could do to you? Think about what it would be like to endure their torment. Imagine Jesus with you during the pain, hanging there with you, helping you to endure. Saying to you, "Surely today you will be with me in paradise." Though the beasts may snarl and rage, they may try to claim us as their own, but in the end, they are just as much under God's control as we are—always six, six, six—never seven. Never as powerful as the lamb that sits upon the throne—the one who was and is and is to come. The one who makes all things new and marks us as God's own people forever.

Amen? Amen!

www.ingramcontent.com/pod-product-compliance
Lightning Source LLC
Chambersburg PA
CBHW052137110526
44591CB00012B/1761